SEEKING IMMORTALITY

CHINESE TOMB SCULPTURE FROM THE SCHLOSS COLLECTION

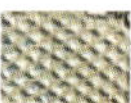

BY JANET BAKER

made possible by

FLUOR DANIEL

THE BOWERS MUSEUM OF CULTURAL ART • SANTA ANA • CALIFORNIA

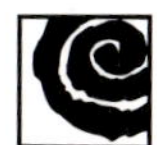

First edition, 1996

Published by the Bowers Museum of Cultural Art,
2002 North Main Street, Santa Ana, CA 92706.

All rights reserved. No part of this publication may be reproduced or transmitted in any form or by any means, electronic or mechanical, including photocopy, recording, or any information storage and retrieval system now known or to be invented, without permission in writing from the publisher, except by a reviewer who wishes to quote brief passages in connection with a review written for inclusion in a magazine, newspaper, or broadcast.

Copyright ©1996 by Museum Associates, The Bowers Museum of Cultural Art. All rights reserved.

Published in conjunction with the exhibition Seeking Immortality: Chinese Tomb Sculpture from the Schloss Collection organized by the Bowers Museum of Cultural Art.

EXHIBITION SCHEDULE:

The Bowers Museum of Cultural Art, Santa Ana, CA.
October 6, 1996 – March 16, 1997.

The Taft Musem, Cincinnati, OH.
September 11 – November 9, 1997.

Frank H. McClung Museum, The University of Tennessee, Knoxville, TN.
December 6, 1997 – March 31, 1998.

ISBN 9633959-5-5

PHOTOGRAPHER: Sarah Wells

DESIGNER: Lynn S. Wu

PRINTER: Pacific Rim International Printing
Hong Kong

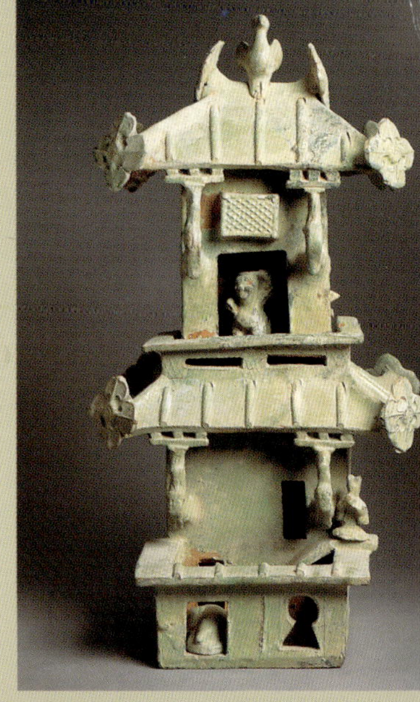

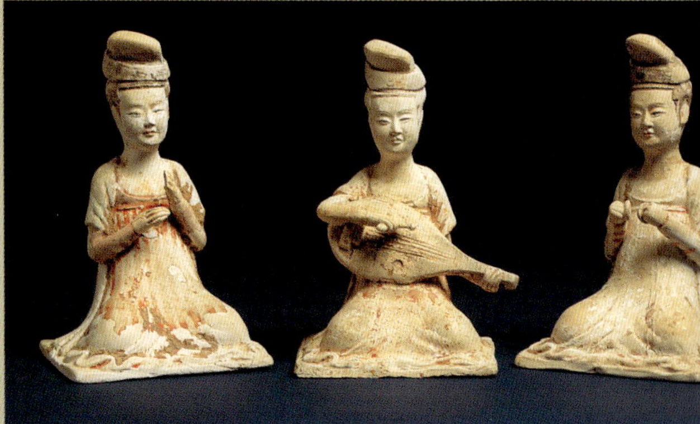

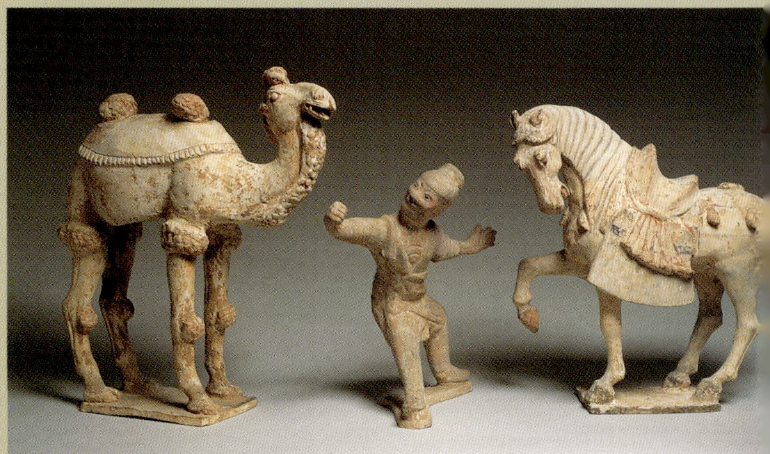

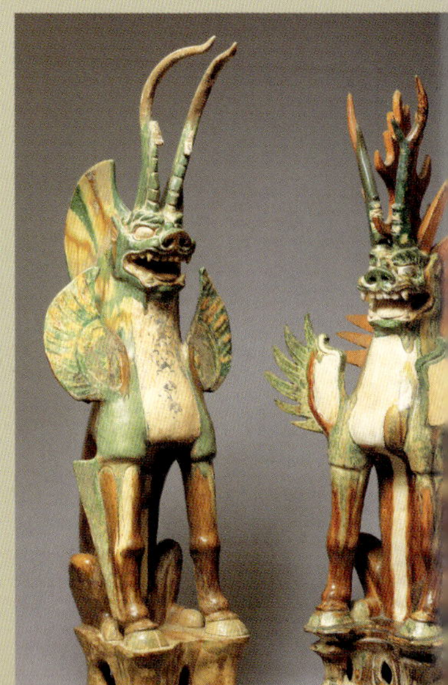

Contents

Foreword

The renowned Schloss Collection of ancient Chinese tomb sculpture consists of almost four hundred valuable examples of funerary art collected over a period of more than forty years by Lillian Schloss and her late husband, Ezekiel. These exquisite ceramic sculptures depict aspects from everyday life in all strata of ancient Chinese society. Clay images ranging from elegantly dressed ladies, dignified officials and stately residences to granaries and farm animals were buried with the dead to accompany and serve them throughout the afterlife.

Lillian and Ezekiel Schloss were among the first collectors of Chinese art to recognize the documentary significance of these tomb sculptures and they became immersed enough in their history to write a book on the subject. By the 1980's, their collection of Chinese funerary sculpture was recognized as the finest private collection of its kind in the United States. Since Ezekiel Schloss's death in 1987, Lillian Schloss has continued to acquire new works and has enlarged the scope of the collection to include pieces from the short-lived but very interesting Sui Dynasty (AD 585-618).

In the past there have been several exhibitions of Chinese tomb sculpture. *The Quest for Eternity*, organized by the Los Angeles County Museum of Art; *Appeasing the Spirits: Sui and Early Tang Tomb Sculpture from the Schloss Collection*, curated by Dr. Baker for exhibition at Hofstra University and SUNY at New Paltz; and *Chinese Tomb Sculpture from the Han Dynasty and the Six Dynasties* at Vassar College treated the tomb sculpture as works of art to be presented either stylistically or chronologically. Dr. Baker is to be congratulated for her scholarship in presenting *Seeking Immortality: Chinese Tomb Sculpture from the Schloss Collection* from a different perspective that takes into account the dramatic changes that took place in China during the millennium from the Han to the Tang Dynasties: a unified empire was forged from scattered kingdoms, newly established trade between China and the outside world resulted in a fascination for anything foreign and new belief systems, most notably Buddhism, took hold and flourished.

Since most paintings from this important time in Chinese history did not survive, tomb sculpture offers a unique glimpse into all aspects of Chinese society including social stratification, ethnic demographics, military practices, agriculture and animal husbandry as well as preferences in costume and hairstyle and advances in architectural design. *Seeking Immortality* is comprised of more than 150 pieces that are grouped as 1) architecture, agriculture and domestic life, 2) social and cultural life, 3) military, sports and transportation, and 4) mythical and supernatural beings. By arranging tomb sculpture by object type rather than stylistically or chronologically, Dr. Baker provides a comprehensive and sensitive insight into the evolution of life in ancient China from the Han through the Tang Dynasties.

The Bowers Museum of Cultural Art is honored and delighted to have had the opportunity to have worked with Lillian Schloss in presenting this important collection. While sharing her treasures in the warmth of her New York apartment, she exuded boundless enthusiasm for her collection and the impending exhibition. Lillian has become a very special friend of the Bowers Museum. She is also to be thanked for believing in Dr. Baker's concept from the onset and for her generous financial support of this catalogue. It is largely through her personal efforts that *Seeking Immortality* will travel to the Taft Museum in Cincinnati and the Frank H. McClung Museum at the University of Tennessee at Knoxville following its presentation at the Bowers. This catalogue would not have been possible without a generous grant from Fluor Daniel, Inc. In addition, special thanks go to Pacific Rim International Printing and the designer, Lynn Wu, for helping to make Dr. Baker's catalogue a reality. Finally, I want to offer my special thanks to the Chinese Cultural Arts Council of the Bowers Museum for their continued support and encouragement.

PETER C. KELLER, PH.D.
Santa Ana, CA
October 1996

Collector's Foreword

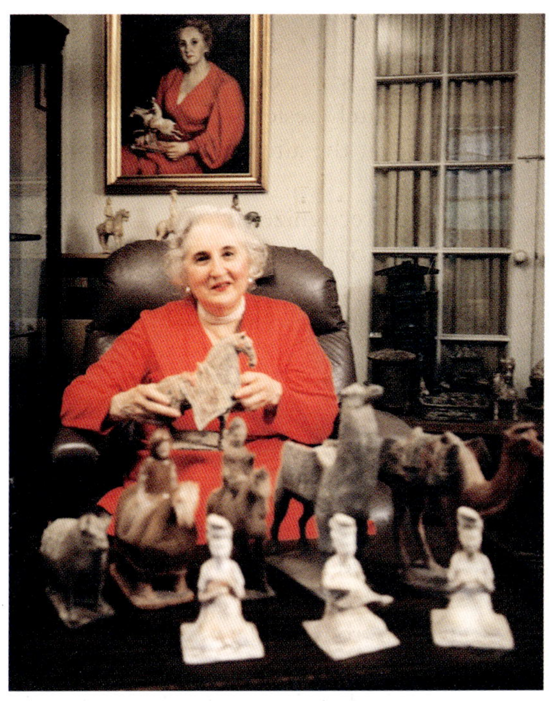

Over the past several years, exhibitions of the Schloss Collection have been focused on particular dynasties. *Seeking Immortality* gives an overview of the entire production of Chinese pottery burial objects from the Han through the Tang Dynasty, that is, during the first millenium of the Christian Era. This objective was achieved by the able and scholarly curator of the exhibition, Dr. Janet Baker, and I am grateful to her for her excellent research and writing of this catalogue. Thoroughly familiar with the collection for a number of years, she selected the most outstanding examples from each period. In this way, contrasts and similarities can be established that allow the viewer to appreciate the transition from one dynasty to the next. To understand the changes in sculptural form, it is helpful to know the social, political and economic status of China during each specific period. These factors influenced the artisans who created these objects, reflecting the society and progress of the empire.

While I appreciate the historical record and the invaluable glimpse into life in each particular time that the burial objects provide, it is their beauty, realism and enormous range of subject matter that I find most appealing. The tombs of ancient China served as time capsules protecting the artifacts until they were discovered in the twentieth century. This is the reason why I love ceramic funerary art and why I have become such an avid collector over the years. It is a passion that has grown with each acquisition and has given me great pride, happiness and satisfaction. I have always tried to acquire pieces of beauty, rarity, quality and unique artistic interpretation. While these ceramic objects were not considered works of art by their makers, they are excellent miniature substitutes for the real people and animals which might have been sacrificed in more ancient times. It seems as if the artisans imbued their creations with so much feeling and liveliness in order to make them better servants to their masters in the next world.

Due to the skillful photography of Sarah Wells, these objects retain their lifelike quality in the catalogue illustrations. Animated and full of vitality, they seem frozen in time, just waiting for a photographer to capture them. The Bowers Museum of Cultural Art is to be congratulated for its long-standing dedication to the cultural achievements in the arts and high standards of scholarship through the leadership of its President, Dr. Peter Keller. I am grateful to him for the opportunity to present my collection at this prestigious institution.

In closing, I would like to mention that my late husband Ezekiel Schloss was the original inspiration for this exhibition. Nearly forty years ago, he was recognized as a pioneer in the appreciation of Chinese tomb sculpture. In 1977, he codified our collection and published his research in his book Ancient Chinese Ceramic Sculpture from Han Through T'ang. Although many of the pieces in that volume have now been sold or donated to museums, new acquisitions have entered the collection as well. Dr. Baker's unique presentation will certainly stimulate interest in my collection and I hope that her efforts will encourage the further appreciation of a great civilization and culture.

LILLIAN SCHLOSS
New York City
October 1996

Preface

By studying civilizations of the past, we can hope to gain a clearer idea of who we are today. By learning more about cultures different from our own, we may acquire a better understanding of other peoples as well as ourselves. In twentieth century America, it is possible to explore the worlds of long ago and far away through such avenues as archaeological exploration, cultural exchange and modern technology. In exhibitions such as "Seeking Immortality: Chinese Tomb Sculpture from the Schloss Collection," we can come face-to-face with images of people who lived more than a thousand years ago on the opposite side of the world. As we look more carefully at these figures, we may come to realize that the lives, hopes, dreams, possessions and pursuits of the ancient Chinese were not so different from our own today. Vast armies of soldiers, sumptuous vehicles, lavish houses, lively entertainers and beautifully dressed men and women all provide silent testimony of the elegant taste for the good life among ancient China's "rich and famous."

Tomb sculpture in China was created solely for the purpose of accompanying the deceased into the afterlife. Designed to serve as replacements for servants and animals, these clay figures have survived virtually intact into the present day, thus allowing us a unique insight into the past. A plethora of these artifacts have entered museum and private collections around the world, while scientific excavation in China in recent decades has provided detailed documentation of dating, provenance and styles. Yet few collectors focused so exclusively on tomb sculpture as Lillian and Ezekiel Schloss. Since the 1950s, the couple pursued their love of Chinese culture by collecting tomb sculpture. Neither of them received any formal training in the field of Chinese art nor did they travel to Asia. Drawing upon the rich cultural resources of New York City, they developed a distinguished collection and became specialists in the topic of tomb sculpture. Mr. Schloss published several exhibition catalogues and a major book on the subject, recognizing the high quality and artistic importance of these works at a time when they were still not widely appreciated.

Since Ezekiel Schloss's death in 1987, Lillian Schloss has continued to acquire new pieces and to exhibit the collection. In 1990, Vassar College staged the exhibition *Into the Afterlife: Han and Six Dynasties Chinese Tomb Sculpture from the Schloss Collection,* curated by Candace J. Lewis. In 1993, a second exhibition *Appeasing the Spirits: Sui and Tang Tomb Sculpture from the Schloss Collection,* curated by me, was shown at Hofstra University and S.U.N.Y. New Paltz. *Seeking Immortality* builds upon the research published in the previous catalogues and places the artifacts in a thematic setting that not only provides the visitor a comprehensive overview of the thousand-year-old tradition of Chinese tomb sculpture but facilitates understanding of the cultural, social, military and technological circumstances of ancient China.

I have had the rare privilege of working closely with Lillian Schloss since 1989. For an emerging scholar, the opportunity to study original works of art is extremely valuable. I will always be grateful for Lillian's faith and support in my research of her collection. Beyond the professional relationship of curator and collector, I am also honored to have Lillian's personal friendship. With her I have shared many wonderful times and met many fascinating people, often in her New York apartment. I treasure my memories of looking at Han Dynasty towers and Tang Dynasty ladies while savoring Lillian's delicious cooking. I hope that *Seeking Immortality* will add to the "joie de vivre" which keeps her so young at heart.

This project would not have come to fruition without the support of Dr. Peter Keller, President of the Bowers Museum of Cultural Art. Over the past four years, Dr. Keller has presented me with professional challenges and opportunities, and I greatly appreciate his interest and assistance. Armand Labbé, Bowers Museum Director of

Research and Collections, has provided counsel in matters of connoisseurship and research. Paul Johnson, Director of Exhibit Design, has created a beautiful installation to display the Schloss Collection at the Bowers Museum. Dr. Patricia House, former Vice-President for Programs and Development, made the appropriate contacts to raise funds to make the exhibition and its related programs a reality. James Stathakis, Vice President of Administration, was most helpful in handling matters of insurance and contracts. Barbara Hanneman, Executive Assistant, kept paperwork and correspondence in order. Brian Langston, Director of Public Relations, worked hard to keep the media, both English and Chinese, informed and involved. Debra Boudreau, Gallery Store Manager, expedited the production and distribution of the catalogue. Teresa Ridgeway, Registrar, and Alice Bryant, Collections Manager, made sure that the Schloss Collection was safely transported and handled all along the way under the expertise of Gander and White Shipping, Inc. of New York. Patricia Korzec, Director of Children's Education and The Bowers Kidseum created activities that brought ancient China alive for the children of Orange County. Allison Miliones, curatorial intern, was a great help with assembling bibliographic materials and numerous other tasks. The Bowers Museum Chinese Cultural Arts Council provided tremendous fund-raising and programmatic support. I wish to thank all members of the Bowers Museum staff for helping to make my first major curatorial project here a success.

Outside of the Bowers Museum, several collegues deserve special mention. Virginia Bower, Judy Chungwa Ho and Donald Wood reviewed the catalogue manuscript and gave welcome input in scholarly matters. I wish to recognize Candace Lewis, curator of the earlier exhibition, *Into the Afterlife*, of the Schloss Han and Six Dynasties material, for her meticulous research in this area of the collection. I also wish to acknowledge the efforts of Daniella Walsh, who contributed her editorial expertise. Finally, I would like to express my gratitude to my husband, Gao Xiao-hua, whose love and respect have given me inspiration and insight over the past twelve years.

In the time I have known Lillian Schloss, I have often regretted that I never had the opportunity to meet Ezekiel Schloss. Since I have read his writings and studied the pieces he has collected, I have begun to feel that in some way I have gotten to know him. In memory of Ezekiel Schloss, his passion for collecting tomb sculpture and his respect for research, I dedicate this catalogue.

JANET BAKER, PH.D.
Santa Ana, CA
October 1996

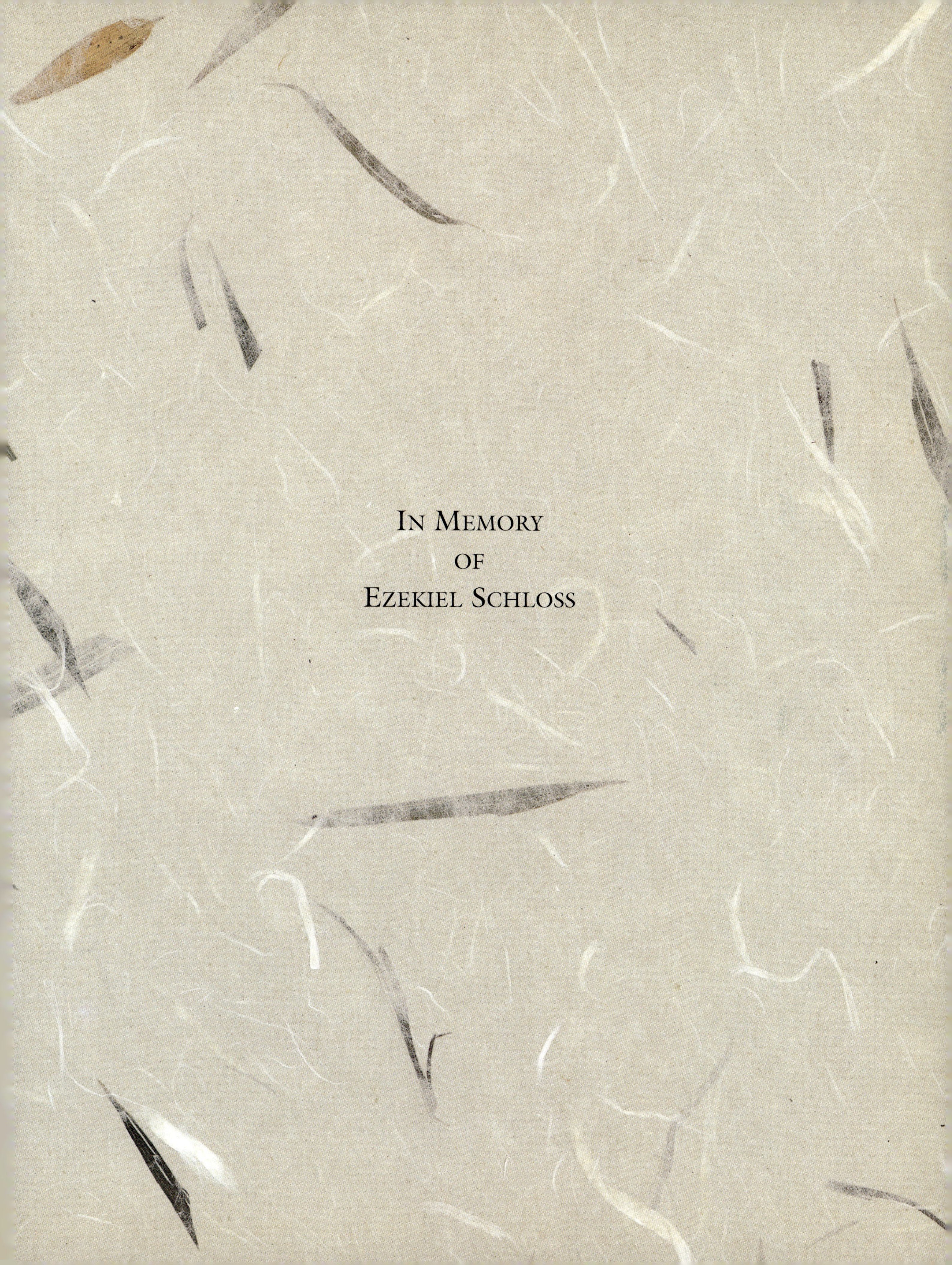

In Memory
of
Ezekiel Schloss

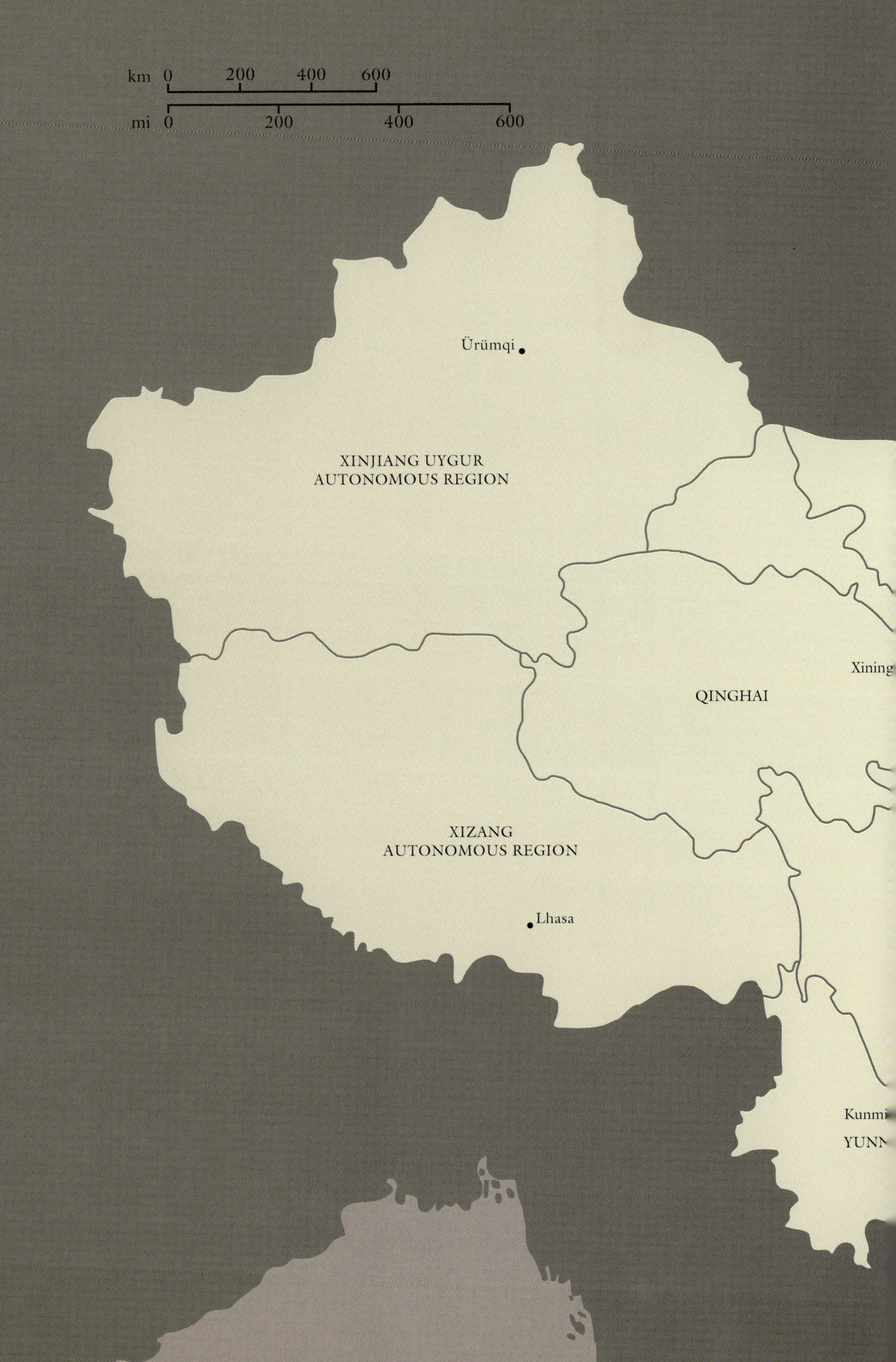
km 0 200 400 600
mi 0 200 400 600
Ürümqi
XINJIANG UYGUR
AUTONOMOUS REGION
QINGHAI
Xining
XIZANG
AUTONOMOUS REGION
Lhasa

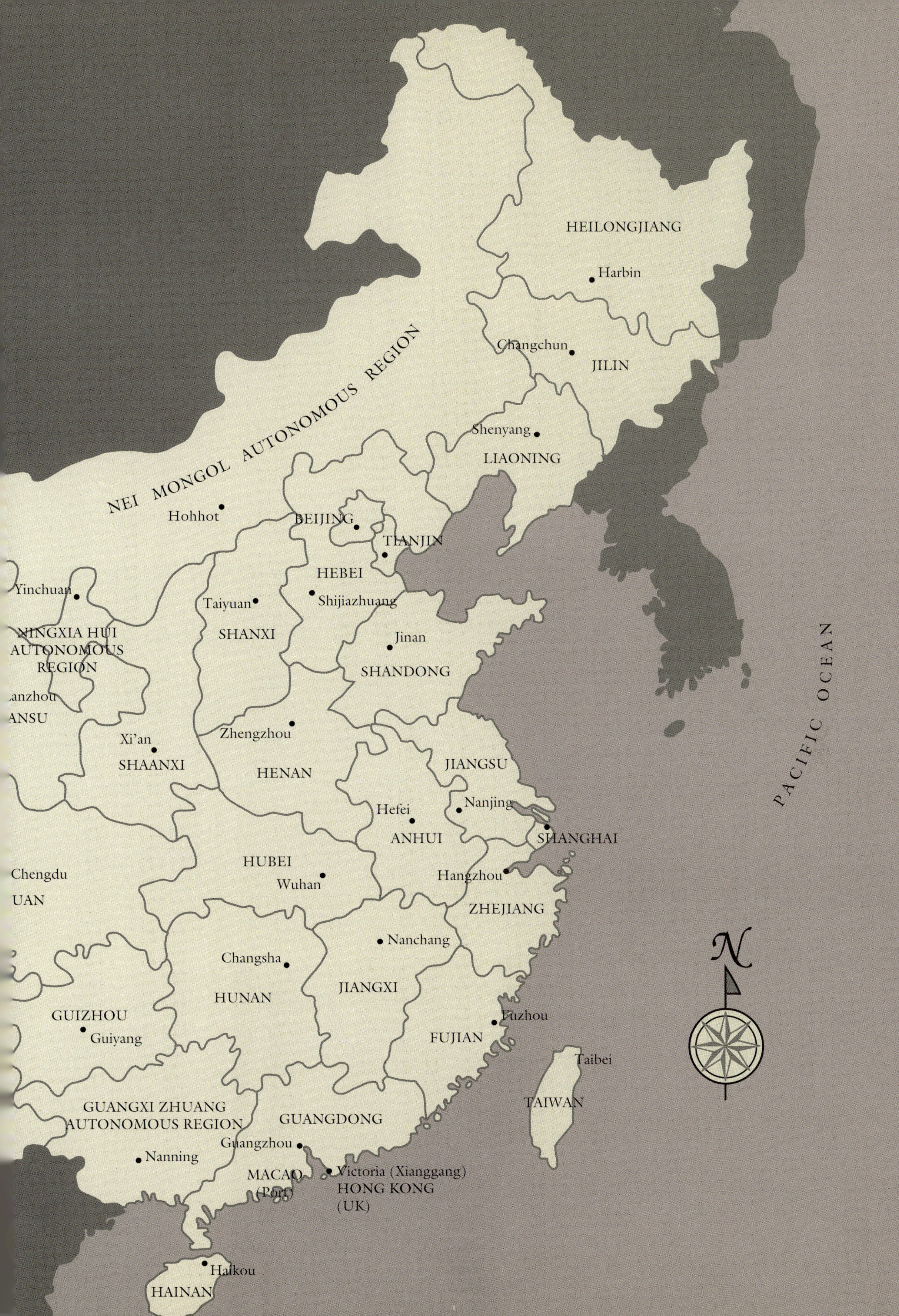

HEILONGJIANG
Harbin
Changchun
JILIN
NEI MONGOL AUTONOMOUS REGION
Shenyang
LIAONING
Hohhot
BEIJING
TIANJIN
HEBEI
Yinchuan
Taiyuan
Shijiazhuang
NINGXIA HUI AUTONOMOUS REGION
SHANXI
Jinan
SHANDONG
anzhou
ANSU
Zhengzhou
Xi'an
SHAANXI
HENAN
JIANGSU
PACIFIC OCEAN
Nanjing
Hefei
ANHUI
SHANGHAI
Chengdu
UAN
HUBEI
Wuhan
Hangzhou
ZHEJIANG
Nanchang
Changsha
JIANGXI
HUNAN
GUIZHOU
Guiyang
Fuzhou
FUJIAN
Taibei
TAIWAN
GUANGXI ZHUANG AUTONOMOUS REGION
GUANGDONG
Guangzhou
Nanning
MACAO (Port)
Victoria (Xianggang)
HONG KONG (UK)
Haikou
HAINAN
N

Chronology

Neolithic Period	**circa 7000~1600 B.C.**
Shang dynasty	**circa 1600~1027 B.C.**
Zhou dynasty	**1027~256 B.C.**
Western Zhou	1027~770 B.C.
Eastern Zhou	770~221 B.C.
Spring and Autumn Period	770~476 B.C.
Warring States Period	475~221 B.C.
Qin dynasty	**221~206 B.C.**
Han dynasty	**206 B.C.~220 A.D.**
Western Han	206 B.C~8 A.D.
Xin (Wang Mang)	8~25 A.D.
Eastern Han	25~220 A.D.
Six Dynasties	**220~589**
Three Kingdoms	
Wei	220~265
Shu	221~263
Wu	220~280
Western Jin	265~317
Southern Dynasties	
Eastern Jin	317~420
Liu Song	420~479
Southern Qi	479-502
Liang	502~557
Chen	557~587
Northern Dynasties	
Sixteen Kingdoms	304~439
Northern Wei	386~535
Eastern Wei	535~550
Western Wei	535~557
Northern Qi	550~557
Northern Zhou	557~581
Sui dynasty	**581~618**
Tang dynasty	**618~906**
Five Dynasties	**906~960**
Song dynasty	**960~1279**
Northern Song	960~1127
Southern Song	1127~1279
Liao dynasty (Khitan)	**916~1125**
Jin dynasty (Jurchen)	**1115~1234**
Yuan dynasty (Mongol)	**1271~1368**
Ming dynasty	**1368~1644**
Qing dynasty (Manchu)	**1644~1911**
Republic	**1912~1949**
Guomingdang (in Taiwan)	1949~
People's Republic	**1949~**

Introduction

Since the founding of the People's Republic of China in 1949, scientifically controlled archaeological investigations have resulted in the discovery of many ancient tombs. The rich contents of these tombs has not only effected a clearer understanding of Chinese funerary practices but of the lives of the Chinese people throughout history. The availability of information pertaining to archaeological work in China to scholars world-wide has brought about an advance in scholarship and an exchange of ideas and methodologies. In recent decades, a spirit of co-operation between China and many other nations has resulted in numerous spectacular travelling exhibitions of recently excavated material, increasing international interest in and understanding of Chinese traditional culture.

The vast majority of objects unearthed from tombs in China are three-dimensional clay sculptures. Known as *mingqi*, these pieces replicate humans, animals and everyday objects used by the deceased and were made strictly for funerary use. [1] Archaeological evidence suggests that the creation of images used in burial practice dates to the Shang Dynasty (1523 - 1028 BC). Wooden and clay figures began to appear during the Zhou Dynasty (770 - 221 BC). The spectacular discovery of the burial site of life-size clay soldiers and horses to accompany the first emperor of a unified China, Qin Shihuangdi (r. 221 - 210 BC), bears testimony to the sophisticated design and production of *mingqi* by that time. During the next one thousand years *mingqi* became a central component of Chinese burial practices. However, by the ninth century *mingqi* were produced in fewer quantities than before, and their quality declined. During the subsequent Liao (907-1125), Song (960-1279) and Yuan (1271-1368) Dynasties, ceramic images were gradually replaced by those made from paper. Paper objects, rather than being buried with the deceased were sent into the afterworld by burning, a custom still practiced in some Chinese communities today. [2]

Information regarding *mingqi* in museum and private collections outside China has been published in books, magazines and catalogues since the early decades of this century. Early writings tended to simply categorize pieces by broad dynastic dates or attempted stylistic analysis. The first major study of ceramic *mingqi*, published in 1977 by Ezekiel Schloss, documented their production and stylistic evolution while validating their aesthetic significance in relation to other Chinese art, especially painting. Currently, questions of provenance, date, function and iconography are being explored by drawing upon recent archaeological data, thus allowing for comparisons between examples in museum and private collections and those found in scientific excavations. Within this context, this exhibition and catalogue illustrate the breadth of tomb sculpture from the Han (206 BC-220 AD) through the Tang (618-906 AD) Dynasties based on an understanding of Chinese mortuary culture, historic background, ceramic production, and archaeological comparison. Most importantly, it illuminates what Chinese tomb sculpture reveals about the important aspects of life in one of the oldest continuous civilizations — social classes, religious beliefs and practices, cultural pursuits, aesthetic preferences, agricultural practices and leisure activities.

Chinese Mortuary Culture and its Relation to the "Three Teachings"

Tomb sculpture is closely linked with Chinese religion and philosophy. In ancient China, beliefs about the afterlife were varied and did not follow any systematic exposition. In order to understand these ideas about the afterlife one must examine both the archaeological evidence as well as the basic tenets of the "three teachings" - Confucianism, Daoism and Buddhism, that governed all aspects of Chinese life. [3]

Confucianism differs in character from Daoism and Buddhism in that it lacks both formal organization and priests or other clergy. Although Confucius, who founded this school of thought in the fifth century BC, was revered as a sage, he never attained the status of a deity. His teachings applied to the conduct of human affairs and life on earth rather than to matters of death or the afterlife. Confucian ethics centered on the morals of loyalty and piety, encompassing hierarchic relationships between emperor and subject, husband and wife, parent and child, as well as interactions among siblings and among friends. Throughout history, no emperor ever found it necessary to reject Confucian teachings, since they had served Chinese society well since Han times on.

While Confucianism took an indifferent position to ghosts and spirits, Daoism centered on a reverence for the spirit world. "Shamanistic" aspects of Daoism included techniques for appeasing spirits and ghosts as well as for the achievement of immortality. But rather than placing itself at odds with Confucianism, Daoism also accepted the hierarchic order of the state. Its founder Laozi became, unlike Confucius, deified and canonized during the Han Dynasty. When Buddhism was introduced from India into China during the Han Dynasty, Daoists also adopted some theological and organizational aspects of Buddhism. Buddhists believed in a higher spirit, that of its founder Sakyamuni Buddha, who is accompanied by different ranks of Buddhas, bodhisattvas (enlightened beings) and disciples. [4] Buddhism gradually became sinified over several centuries, gaining popular and political acceptance during the Six Dynasties period. Buddhist pilgrims, along with Silk Route merchants, were a vehicle for the importation of foreign thought, goods and art, which influenced virtually all aspects of Tang culture.

Regarding the afterlife, all three belief systems held that the realms of earthly life and the hereafter were continuous and related. The Confucian concepts of filial piety and ancestor worship were of primary importance, dictating that the deceased remain the head of the family while familial responsibilities were maintained. However, the development of funerary art and architecture did not only serve to honor deceased ancestors but also to appease spirits and ghosts. Daoist belief in the power of the spirits of the dead meant that failure to fulfill funerary obligations could result in malevolent retribution. Daoists believe that a living person is endowed with two souls: the first is the *hun* or "light" soul that gives a person the spark of life and intelligence. It is ascribed to the *yang* or active male realm and ascends to heaven, becoming a spirit or *shen*. The second soul is called the *po* or "heavy" soul and is ascribed to the passive female realm, the *yin*. After death, the po returns to earth as the deceased's ghost or *gui*. While these elements are united in the physical body during life, the *hun* and *po* separate after death. Sacrifices and ceremonies were designed to ensure the *hun's* safe passage to heaven while the *po* was entreated to remain in the tomb with the deceased's body, lest it become a wandering and malevolent *gui*. [5]

In ancient China the tomb was a meeting place for the two worlds as well as a gate to the afterlife. The structure also served as a place where the living could communicate with the souls of their ancestors and bring offerings to sustain the *gui* which had remained there, surrounded by images to ward off evil and replicas of the accoutrements the departed had been accustomed to in life. While the tombs were filled with food supplies, clothing, furniture, dishes and the requisite *mingqi*, the walls bore painted scenes from the life of the deceased, illustrations of mythological tales and depictions of the immortals. Preparations for a tomb were begun well before an individual's death. Preparations for an emperor's tomb, for example, were begun in the second year of his reign. [6] An increasing profusion of objects in the tombs led to the development of sumptuary laws specifying the types and quantities of grave goods that could be interred based on the social rank of the deceased. From the emperor on down, each member of Chinese society was buried according to prescribed code, thus insuring that the zeal of filial piety on the part of the living would not lead to inappropriate ostentation or bankruptcy. [7]

The writings of Xunzi, a follower of Confucius, chronicle the growing importance of funerary rituals as signs of respect and concern for the deceased making their journey across the threshold of death. Xunzi wrote "the rites of the dead can be performed only once for each individual, and never again. They are the last occasion upon which the subject may fully express respect for his ruler, the son express respect for his parents...In the funeral rites, one adorns the dead as though they were still living, and sends them to the grave with forms symbolic of life."[8]

Historical Background of the Han, Six Dynasties, Sui and Tang Periods

In the late third century BC, the First Emperor of Qin, Shihuangdi, unified China's vast regions and large population into a centralized, autocratic empire. Subsequent dynasties followed the model of government established by the Qin emperor. All decision-making power was placed in the Emperor's hands and there were no other power structures, legislatures or theological rulers. [9]

The four hundred years of the Han Dynasty (206 BC - 220 AD) really encompassed three periods: the Western Han (206 BC - 8 AD), when the capital was located in Chang'an (modern-day Xi'an), the Wang Mang interregnum (8 - 25 AD), and the Eastern Han (25 - 220 AD), when the capital was moved to Luoyang. Building on the unified empire they inherited from the Qin, the Han emperors expanded China's territory through numerous border wars, established a bureaucratic structure to administer the monarchy, improved agriculture and other technologies, and united the various ethnic peoples under the Confucian state ideology.

The decline of the Han empire, due to popular uprisings and revolts, culminated in the flight of the emperor and the burning of the palaces, temples and houses of Luoyang. The four hundred years of disunity and warfare which followed stand in dramatic contrast to the previous four centuries of stable and peaceful Han rule. Even the name given to the turbulent period, Six Dynasties, gives testimony to its divided nature. Petty kingdoms struggled against one another to achieve control over different regions of the once-vast Chinese territory. Warfare, disease, social unrest, political chaos and disillusionment with the Confucian ideals of statecraft resulted in the ascendancy of Buddhism during the Six Dynasties.

A tribe from the northern border areas of China, the Toba Wei, formed the most powerful state and provided imperial patronage of Buddhism. As the rulers expanded their control into the central plains of China, they also spread the influence of Buddhism which brought about the creation of splendid temple complexes. In the late sixth century, China was reunited again under the ruling house of the Sui. The first emperor of the Sui Dynasty (581 - 618) established Buddhism as the state religion, reorganized the economy, and created cultural homogeneity among the former regional factions. However, under the rule of his successor, this short dynasty collapsed due to combination of political corruption and rivalry and disastrous border wars.

The succeeding Tang Dynasty (618 - 907) was built upon the foundations established by the first Sui emperor. A succession of astute emperors in the seventh and eighth centuries ushered in and sustained one of the most brilliant epochs of Chinese civilization. While their military genius and civil administration contributed to the political stability and economic prosperity of the Tang Dynasty, the emperors' tastes, fashions and social habits became lasting influences on the development of Chinese culture during succeeding dynasties. Successful military campaigns, patronage of Buddhism, and subsequent religious pilgrimages along with the development of new trade routes linking them with peoples to the west led to the development of a cosmopolitan population. A strong interest in exotic arts, goods and fashions from abroad became the hallmark of the splendid Tang twin capitals at Chang'an and Luoyang. Chang'an was the larger and more important since it served as the eastern terminus of the great trans-Asian Silk Route and was also the location of the main imperial palaces.

Tomb Design and Construction - Han to Tang Dynasties

Beginning in the first and second centuries AD, the architectural design of Chinese tombs built during the Han, Six Dynasties, Sui and Tang eras was standardized to a degree by the codification of funeral and mourning practices. The two important considerations that determined tomb design were the performance of burial rites within the tomb and the burial of husbands and wives in a single chamber. This meant that the

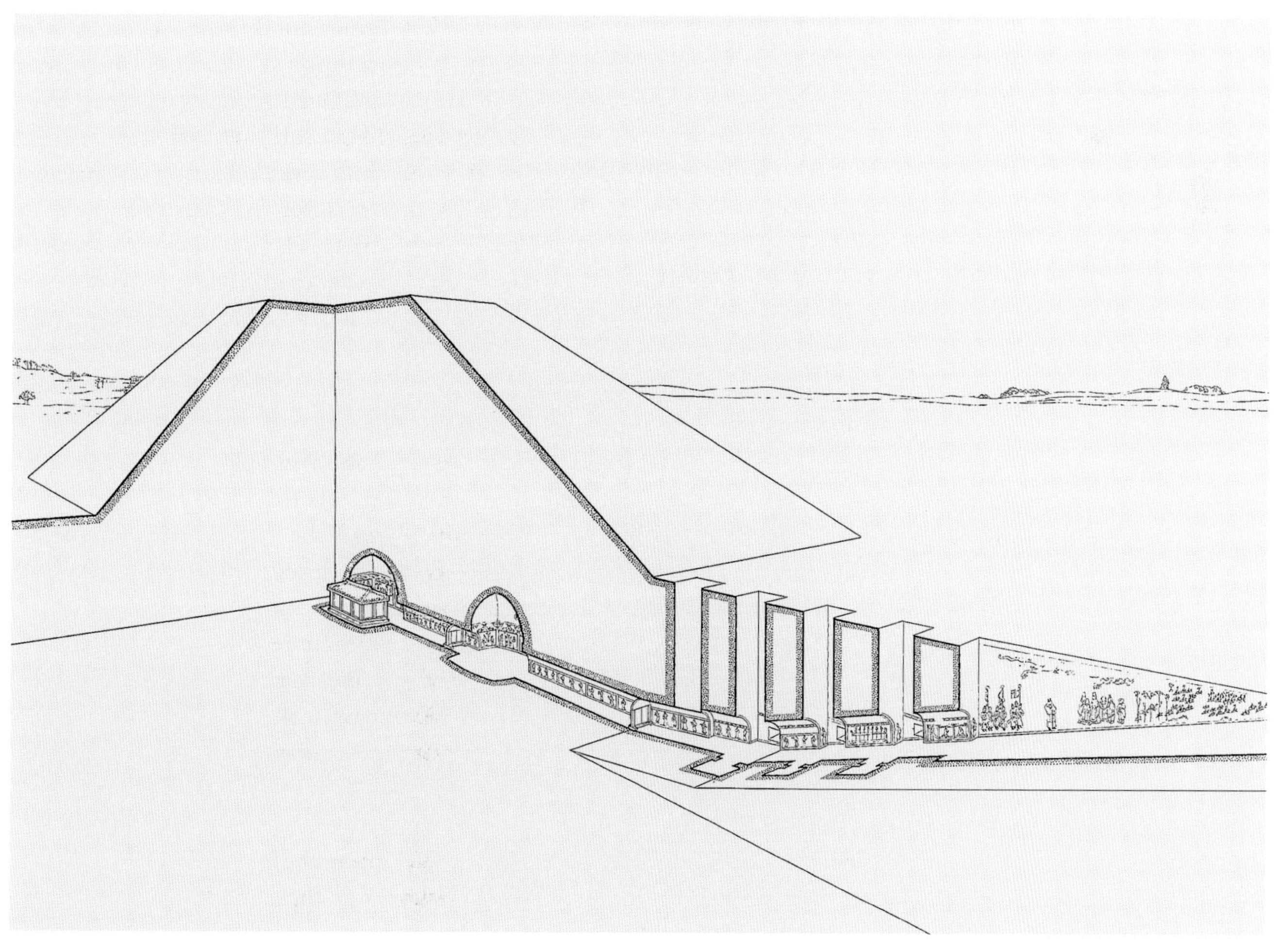

Cross section of the Tang Dynasty tomb of Li Xian, Prince Zhanguai, Qian County, Shaanxi Province. From Tang Li Xian Mu Bihua, 1974.

chamber had to remain intact for some years after the first internment, be large enough to accomodate at least two coffins and accompanying grave goods and allow for the re-opening and re-sealing of the tomb. Though Han Dynasty tomb builders experimented with different materials and designs, a basic working tomb design had evolved by the sixth century. A sloping entrance ramp led to a door at the entrance to a square cave-like chamber dug into the soil and enforced with ceramic bricks for permanence. During the seventh century, construction incorporated niches for the placement of *mingqi* and vertical shafts for light and air (during construction). By that time, elaborate murals were added as well. Early eighth century funerary architecture is exemplified by the imperial Tang tombs which had evoloved into vast funerary parks located in the mountains outside the capital in Chang'an. Each Tang emperor's tomb was accompanied by a number of satellite tombs occupied by the imperial family and members of the court. Above ground, these necropolises were approached by long "spirit paths" marked by monumental stone sculpture and magnificent sacrificial halls. [10]

Materials and Methods of Production of *Mingqi*

The majority of *mingqi* were produced by mold casting, a technique known to Chinese craftsmen as early as 1500 BC when it was used during the Shang Dynasty to create bronze vessels. Single and multiple molds used in in the production of *mingqi* combined with creative hand modelling resulted in a greater variety and complexity of objects. Well-fitting molds allowed assembly-line production of identical three-dimensional figures by joining front and back molds by a center seam. For more complex figures such as horses or camels, various appendages were mold cast separately and attached to the main body with the support of armatures. Finishing touches such as ornamental relief decoration were also mold cast and attached separately. Facial details and other incised lines were added by hand. [11]

Various clays and glazes used throughout the centuries in the production of *mingqi* were selected by regional workshops. Most information regarding *mingqi* production is based on tomb findings since few kiln sites, except several Tang Dynasty sites at Gongxian, near Luoyang and at Tongchuan, near the western capital of Changan, have been discovered. In the Han Dynasty, artisans began to cast pieces in gray clay which was then covered by white slip and painted after firing. Other Han *mingqi* were made from red clay that was either left unglazed or covered with an iridescent brown or green lead glaze which seems to have been invented in the first century AD. During the subsequent Six Dynasties period Northern Wei sculptors painted unglazed gray clay with pigments while their counterparts in south China graced white stoneware pieces with celadon glazes. During the latter sixth century, especially during the short Sui Dynasty, a fine white kaolinic clay body covered with a translucent or creamy white glaze combined with unglazed pigments was prevalent. The addition of white slip or coating under the glaze served to seal the porous surface and brighten the colors. This in turn provided an ideal ground for the brilliant polychrome glazes, often called "three-colored" or *sancai* because of the suffused combinations of brilliant green, yellow, brown or blue hues, which flourished during the late seventh and early eighth centuries. During the mid-Tang period, *mingqi* with red clay bodies covered with white slip and pigments also appeared. [12]

Repertoire & Style of *Mingqi*

The subject matter of *mingqi* chosen for production usually reflected Chinese social circumstances and religious beliefs of a particular period. In the Han Dynasty, for example, architectural and agrarian objects such as large towers, farmhouses, pigpens, stoves and granaries were prevalent. This reflected the four centuries of peaceful rule over a prosperous society with an agrarian focus and composed largely of a peasant population. During the subsequent Six Dynasties period, social turmoil caused by the warring factions of the north and south gave rise to a large military buildup. Images of soldiers, armored equestrians and foreign mercenaries replaced the domestic subjects of the Han. Fantastic animals and otherworldly guardian beasts testified to the influx of new spiritual concepts, including Buddhism. Under the consolidation of the Sui and Tang empire, by contrast, a flourishing international economy and cultural expansiveness led to the creation of *mingqi* replicating exotic entertainers, aristocratic equestrians, thoroughbred horses and camels. A familiar array of *mingqi* depicting officials, women, attendants, servants, domestic animals such as chicken, pigs, sheep and dogs, along with several types of therianthropic creatures, which combined human and animal characteristics, remained constant throughout the centuries. While the majority of *mingqi* are modelled on recognizable forms, there are also others which are clearly fantastic, often integrating human and animal characteristics. Most of these supernatural types represent spirits, legendary beings, guardians and imaginary creatures of an auspicious nature.

The Schloss collection contains a dramatic variety of *mingqi* which represent the sculptural styles prevalent throughout the millenium. In the past the tendency was to date objects according to dynastic origins even though the emergence of an artistic style did not necessarily coincide with political change. Thus, a piece in the Schloss collection can be more accurately dated if it is compared to published archaeological examples rather than "Six Dynasties" or "Tang." Archaeological finds of *mingqi* can also aid in the verification or dating of Chinese technological innovations.

The earliest Han Dynasty pieces in the collection are distinguished by flowing, linear silhouettes and a minimum of details. Although the figures are naturalistic, the artists preferred to stress a sense of movement, liveliness and vigor rather than an exact replication of an image. Such animation sometimes took on a humorous or comic feeling. Although the Han pieces tend to be small, their form and proportions convey a sense of monumentality. This sculptural quality was maintained well into the first century of the Six Dynasties period, after which the stylistic influence from Buddhist art took over.

Mingqi produced during the Northern Wei period were stylized to convey a feeling of dignity and elegance. Human forms tended to be tall and slender with small heads and gently smiling faces. An emphasis on specific, quite naturalistic details combined with exaggerations and linear rhythms began to emerge, creating a balanced tension. Even though some figures seem awkward or rigid, the majority convey a feeling of ethereal grace, tenderness and refinement that echoes Buddhist sculpture of the period.

During the sixth century a gradual yet major transformation of style occurred that is marked by solidity of mass, renewed vigor of pose and an unprecendented realism of form and detail. These trends were paralleled by rapid technological changes. *Mingqi* of the late sixth and early seventh century were infused with a new sense of individuality and emotional expression in movement, gesture and facial features. Poses suggesting objects held or manipulated in the hands, singing and dancing and, among animal *mingqi*, galloping horses provide a sense of *shengdong* (living movement) not seen since six centuries prior, during the Han Dynasty. A sensitive definition of body parts and their interaction suggests a softer and more flexible sense of sculptural form.

Tang funerary art reached its peak during the late seventh century when artists used multiple molds and brilliant "three-colored" glazes to achieve a fully-developed sense of three-dimensionality, realistic action and accurate portrait likeness. By the early decades of the eighth century, a close study of human models, an observation of the subject's psychological character and a general interest in minute detail becomes evident. However, this baroque style was short-lived and by the mid-eighth century "three-colored" *mingqi* were rarely produced. Furthermore, political unrest caused a decline of lavish burials at the imperial court. Intricate realism was supplanted by stylization of form combined with a minimum of detail, as exemplified by the "fat ladies" popular in the later Tang period, whose flowing, volumetric curves were modelled in unglazed red clay.

Archaeological discoveries of the past few decades have yielded tombs of later dynasties filled with *mingqi* providing evidence that by the ninth century the quality and quantity of the artifacts declined dramatically. Wooden or metal figures were eventually replaced by paper *mingqi* when, in later dynasties, funerary customs changed and ceramic production shifted to utilitarian objects for the court and the upper classes. [13]

NOTES:

1. The question of the exact meaning of the word *mingqi* appears to have no clear answer. It has often been translated as "articles of the spirit", but this interpretation depends on what characters in Chinese are utilized. The character for *qi* is universally agreed to be the generic term meaning items, wares or articles. The word *ming* varies, with most non-Chinese scholars using the character meaning bright or shining, or refers the Ming Dynasty. In some Chinese writings, however, another character is used, whose meaning appears more appropriate to the meaning and function of *mingqi*. This character refers generally to that which is dark an obscure and specifcally to anything associated with the deceased, the underworld and the afterlife. One theory is that the character meaning bright was substituted for the one associated with the afterlife or underworld as a way of avoiding unlucky or inauspicious association. This author relies on the meanings given to these two characters in Mathew's Chinese Dictionary.

2. Wang Renbo, "General Comments on Chinese Funerary Sculpture," The Quest for Eternity, pp. 39-61.

3. For a fascinating discussion of early Chinese concepts of eternity and death, see David N. Keightley, "The Quest for Eternity in Ancient China: The Dead, Their Gifts, Their Names," Ancient Mortuary Traditions of China, pp. 12-24.

4. For a general introduction to the "three teachings" and their importance in ancient China, see Robert L. Thorp, Son of Heaven: Imperial Arts of China, pp. 21-28.

5. Albert E. Dien, "Chinese Beliefs in the Afterlife," The Quest for Eternity, p. 3. For a more in-depth study, see Michael Lowe, Chinese Ideas of Life and Death, chapter three, "The Life Hereafter."

6. For a general discussion of beliefs concerning the afterlife and their pictorial representation, see Wu Hung, "Myths and Legends in Han Funerary Art," Stories From China's Past, pp. 72-81. See also the discussion of funerary imagery in Martin Powers, Art and Political Expression in Early China, pp. 50-61. In addition to placing *mingqi* and other artifacts in the tomb, the Chinese of the Han Dynasty also attempted to preserve the corpse by encasing it in suits made of jade; see Robert L. Thorp, pp. 179-180.

7. Robert L. Thorp, p. 170.

8. Burton Watson, trans., Hsun Tzu (Xun Zi): Basic Writings, pp. 97-105 passim.

9. Robert L. Thorp, pp. 21-25.

10. Robert L. Thorp, "The Qin and Han Imperial Tombs and the Development of Mortuary Architecture," The Quest for Eternity, pp. 17-37. For a detailed study of the evolution of tomb design from the Han to the Tang Dynasties, see Mary L. Fong, "Antecedents of Sui-Tang Burial Practices in Shaanxi," pp. 147-159. For a detailed study of the monumental sculpture placed above ground, see Ann Paludan, The Chinese Spirit Road.

11. Ezekiel Schloss, Ancient Chinese Ceramic Sculpture From Han Through T'ang, pp. 47-49.

12. Ibid., pp. 50-51. See also the discussion of Tang ceramic techniques discussed in Ezekiel Schloss, "Questions and Answers About Tang," Significant Aspects of Early Chinese Ceramic Arts, pp. 38-44. For an updated analysis of clay bodies and glazes based on recent archaeological finds, see George Kuwayama, "The Sculptural Development of Ceramic Funerary Figures in China," The Quest for Eternity, pp. 63-93.

13. For a detailed discussion of the sculptural style of *mingqi* from Han to Tang, see George Kuwayama, "The Sculptural Development of Ceramic Funerary Figures in China," The Quest for Eternity, pp. 63-93.

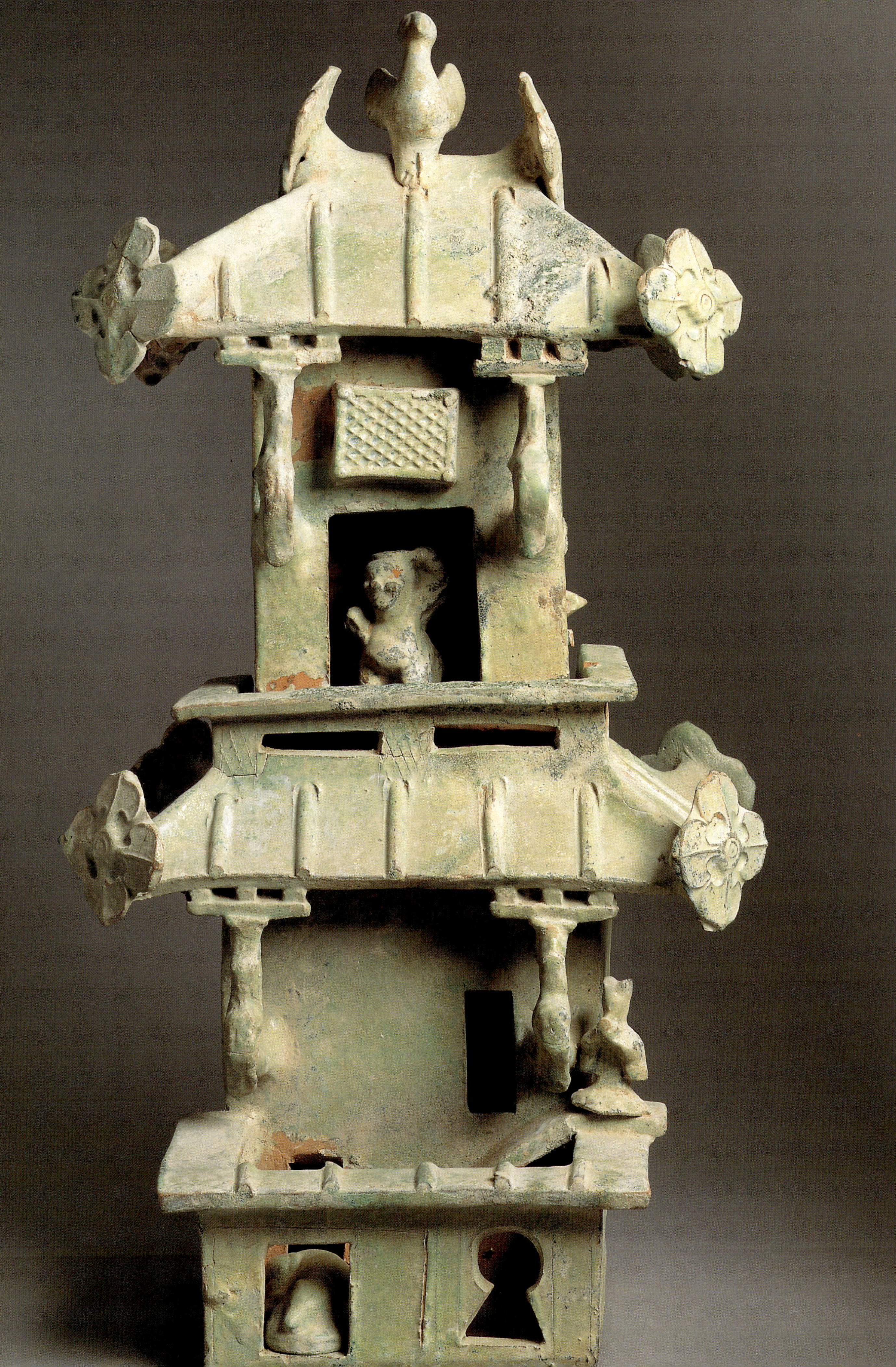

Architecture, Agriculture and Daily Life

Architecture

Virtually nothing survives of the cities and towns of the Han and Tang periods in China except some remains of walls and terraces made of rammed earth. Unlike ancient Egyptians, Greeks and Romans, ancient Chinese builders used perishable materials such as wood and earth for the majority of the civilization's architecture. Much of what has been pieced together about early Chinese architecture and urban design comes from written texts, scant remains, tomb chamber designs, and *mingqi*.

The Han capital city at Chang'an was surrounded by rivers and sheltered by mountains. Under the reign of Emperor Han Wudi palace complexes were constructed as personal residences and as symbols of authority. Surrounded by walls, the palace structures and gardens were set apart from the rest of the city which was encircled by its own set of walls. This concept of delineating royal and city spaces remained a standard feature of Chinese urban planning until the twentieth century.

From archaeological excavations of the residential and palatial remains in Chang'an, it is clear that the Han emperors held multi-storied buildings in high esteem. Their purpose was to provide a link between the world of mortals and the realm of the immortals, thus playing an important part in the expression of imperial power. From the historical records, we know that some of the towers constructed by Han Wudi reached over one hundred meters in height, and were ornamented with metal, semi-precious stones, jade and silk. [1]

The clearest idea of what such buildings may have actually looked like comes from tombs of the Han period excavated all over China. While the tombs are underground replicas of the deceased's living quarters, inscriptions indicate that the interred were wealthy landowners or members of the nobility. Some of the tombs are multi-chambered constructions formed of tiles impressed with images of houses, markets, scenes of domestic life and activities such as grain hulling and fishing. *Mingqi* towers and houses offer a wealth of detail about Han period architecture. Other *mingqi* portray equipment such

Facing page: Tower (Object #2)

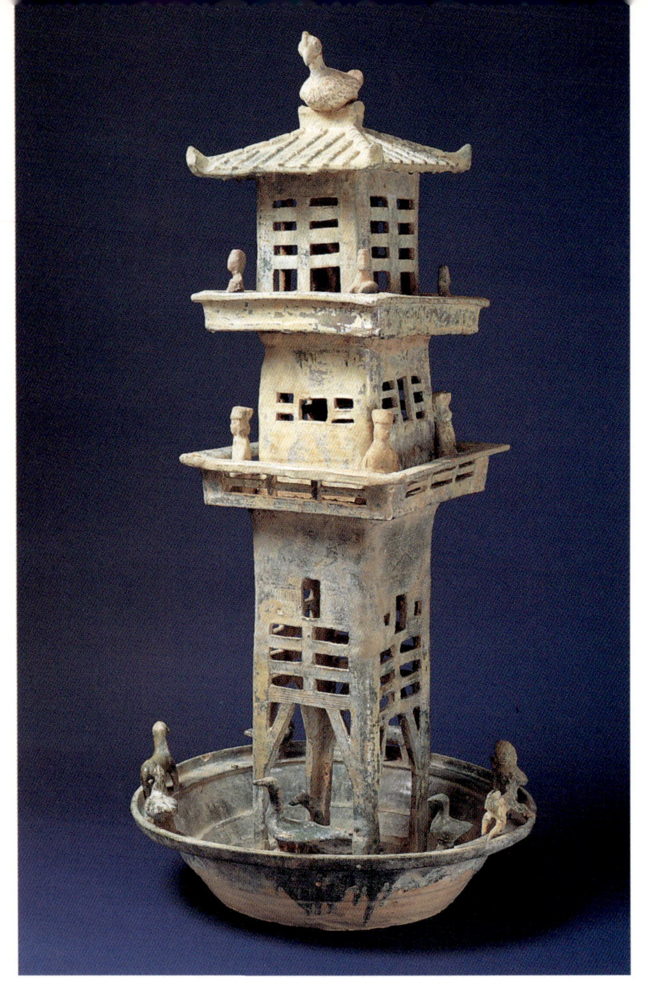

1.
TOWER WITH MOAT
(OBJECT #1)

as stoves, granaries, pigsties and wells give a rich portrayal of every-day life in Han period China. Although scholars continue to debate as to the extent to which *mingqi* represent actual Han architecture, they generally agree upon the existence of towers during that period.

Towers are among the largest and most impressive of architectural *mingqi*. Some appear to have been used for defense during the late Han period, when private armies and armories increased due to political unrest and factional power struggles. Many defensive towers are are placed in a shallow basin signifying a surrounding moat. They are identifiable by figures armed with crossbows standing on the upper verandas. However, if a tower features a crossbow hung up over the doorway, the structure was probably used for non-defensive purposes.

Towers also seem to have been prestigious locations for parties and social gatherings. Figures peering out of windows or posed along the porches and eaves of the different stories include musicians, acrobats, and officials, suggesting that a celebration or other festive gathering is taking place. Some of these "pleasure pavilions" are also surrounded by moats filled with replicas of fish, frogs, turtles and geese. [2] It has been suggested that the celebrations in the towers might be funerary feasts for the deceased buried in the tomb. [3] (Figure 1)

While certain features of the towers, such as the number of stories and specific designs vary, they all bear design elements that were probably standard in Han architecture. A raised platform supporting a timber post-and-lintel structure topped by a tiled and ornamented roof with overhanging eaves and upturned edges characterised basic Chinese architectural design. In order to provide adequate support for such a roof, the *dougong* bracketing system was invented, which is essentially a square block atop the corner supporting columns. This block bears a series of outward jutting arms which supports the overhanging weight of the roof, and is counterbalanced by intersecting transverse arms parallel to the wall planes and long cantilevered arms which descend from the inner superstructure. (Figure 2)

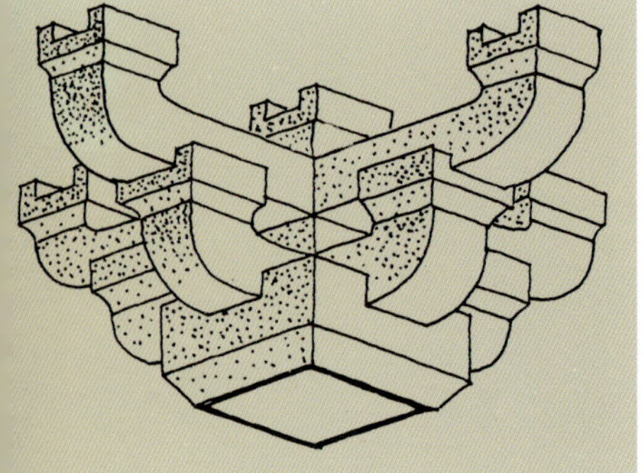

2.
DIAGRAM OF *DOUGONG* BRAKETING SYSTEM. FROM A PICTORAL HISTORY OF CHINESE ARCHITECTURE (M.I.T., 1984).

Virtually all Chinese buildings from the Han period to the present day were designed with this basic support system, although it was varied and refined throughout the centuries. [4] For example, instead of the overhanging roof, some buildings had a gabled or hip roof. In addition to towers, other buildings such as farmhouses, animal pens and granaries were all constructed within the same architectural guidelines during the Han period. (Figure 3) While there was undoubtedly regional variation in style, such distinctions are in many cases still unclear. However, a basic division between northern and southern architectural style appears in the *mingqi* excavated: tall multi-storied towers were mostly found in Han tombs in north China while single-story farmhouses or courtyard style residences were found in southern tombs. [5]

3.
Barn with dog
(Object #8)
Farmhouse with two figures
(Object #9)

Agriculture and Domesticated Animals

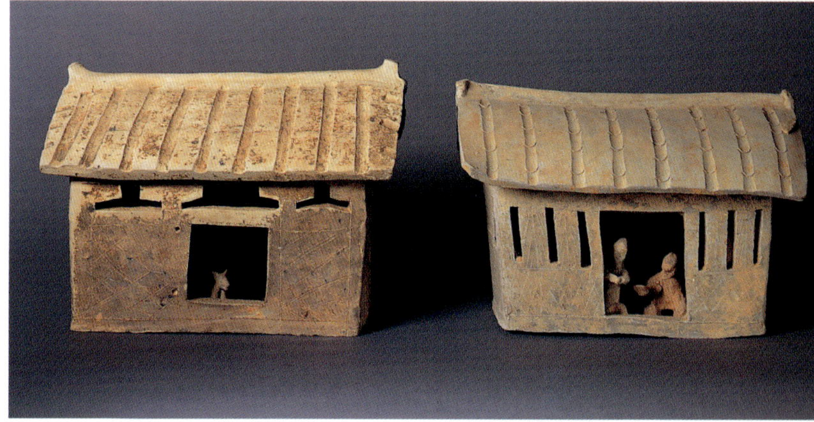

The Han Dynasty brought about great achievements in agriculture, irrigation and water conservancy and the invention of more efficient tools. Waterways were brought under control to prevent flooding and to facilitate the shipment of grain, a mainstay of the tax system. Fields were tilled with swingplows that featured an iron cutting edge and were drawn by oxen. Driven by one or two men, these plows were in widespread use by the second century BC. [6] The development of hand-operated rotary millstones, pounders worked via a system of levers, winnowers with rotary wings and hydraulic mills led to great advances in the processing of grain. Such relatively sophisticated technology combined with nationalized industries and standards helped to assure a stable agrarian economy during the Han period. [7] (Figure 4)

Animal *mingqi* such as pigs, chickens, geese, ducks, sheep, oxen and dogs bear testimony to the importance of raising and herding livestock in ancient China. While dogs were kept mainly as protective beasts, a variety of hounds imported from Central Asia were in demand for imperial hunting expeditions during the Tang period. An inextricable part of Chinese daily life, animals also took on symbolic meaning. The dog, for example, was thought of as the embodiment of fidelity. Although the pig had been domesticated for at least a thousand years prior to the Han period, most *mingqi* depict wild pigs or boars bearing tusks and manes. Shown in painted pottery of the Han engaged in combat with other animals, wild boars symbolize the wealth of the forest since their flesh could be consumed and their bristles manufactured into brushes. The ram or sheep, domesticated for its meat and wool, is also a symbol of filial respect, since it is said to kneel when taking its mother's milk. At the other end of the spectrum it is an emblem of retired life and a pun on the word for "good fortune". While chickens served mainly as a source of food, the rooster's crowing was associated with a number of auspicious occurences in China, such the scaring away of a ghost. Fraught with such symbolic importance the pig, sheep, chicken and dog are among the twelve animals of the Daoist chronological zodiac. [8]

4.
Scene of grain hulling with human figure and dog
(Object #15)
Cylindrical granary
(Object #16)

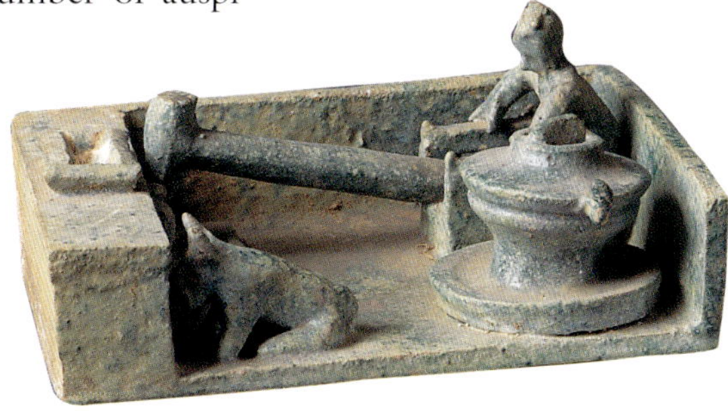

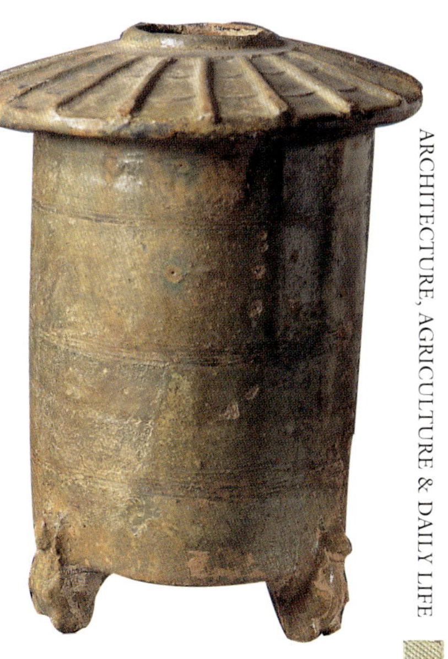

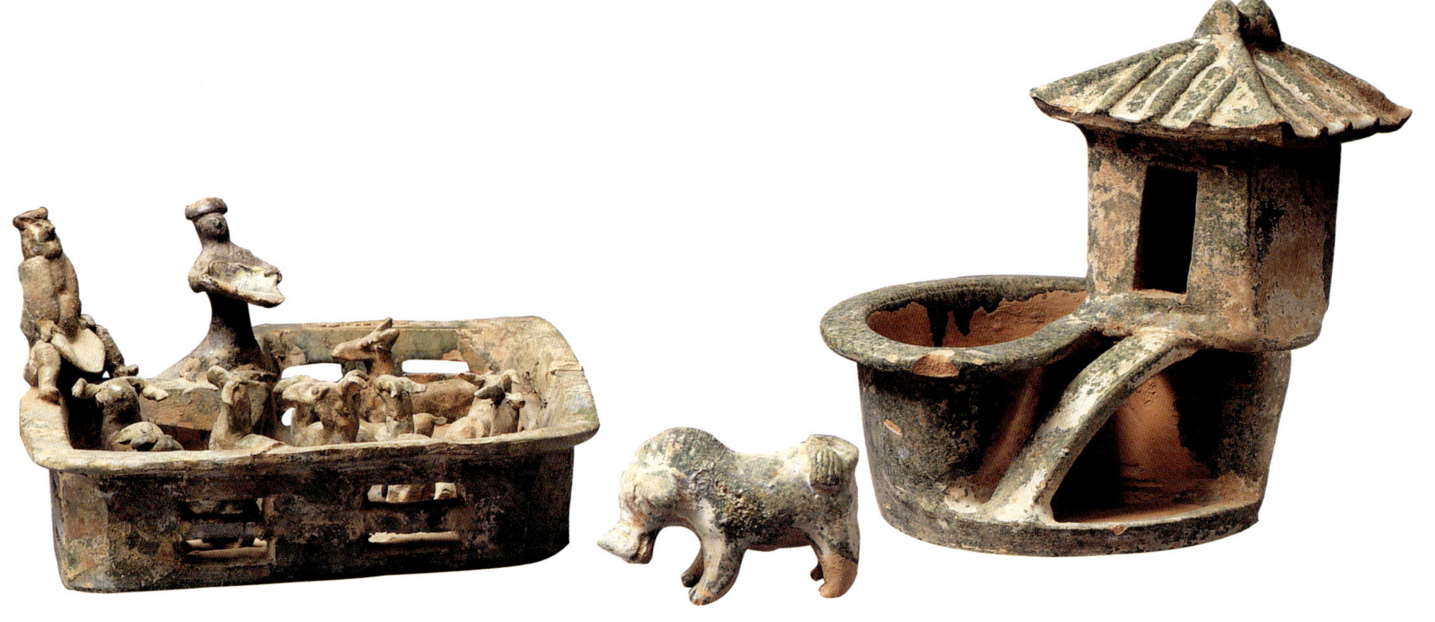

5.
Pen with goats being fed
(Object #12)
Pig
(Object #13)
Pig pen with privy
(Object #14)

These four beasts, plus the horse and the ox, were collectively known as the "six domesticated animals" as early as the second century BC. and the expression "may the six domesticated animals thrive" is still used in rural areas to invoke prosperity for householders moving into new premises. [9] (Figures 5-8)

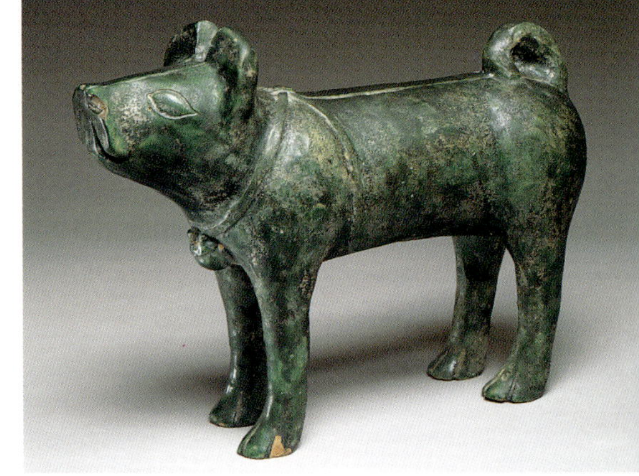

6.
Watchdog (Object #21)

Daily Life Activities

Han Dynasty tombs in particular were filled with *mingqi* related to domestic life, including lamps, stoves, wellheads, incense burners and a variety of containers. These objects reflect an intense interest in the preparation of food for both daily consumption and special festivals and ceremonies. (Figure 9) Tomb tiles of Han date show people tending stoves in the marketplace, along with restaurant customers milling about. The Han stove was usually rectangular with a door at one end for loading firewood, a surface with two burner holes and sometimes a chimney at the other end. (Figure 10) The surface of the stove shows a variety of foodstuffs, such as fish and meat, as well as cooking utensils rendered in relief. The domestic water supply often came from a well, hence the inclusion of *mingqi* wellheads in tombs.

In traditional China, the annual cycle of the agrarian calendar was punctuated by feast-days and sacrificial offerings to the ancestors. At celebrations of the New Year Festival, sacrifices

7.
Ox with trappings
(Object #22)
Chewing dog
(Object #23)
Reclinging dog
(Object #24)
Ram
(Object #25)

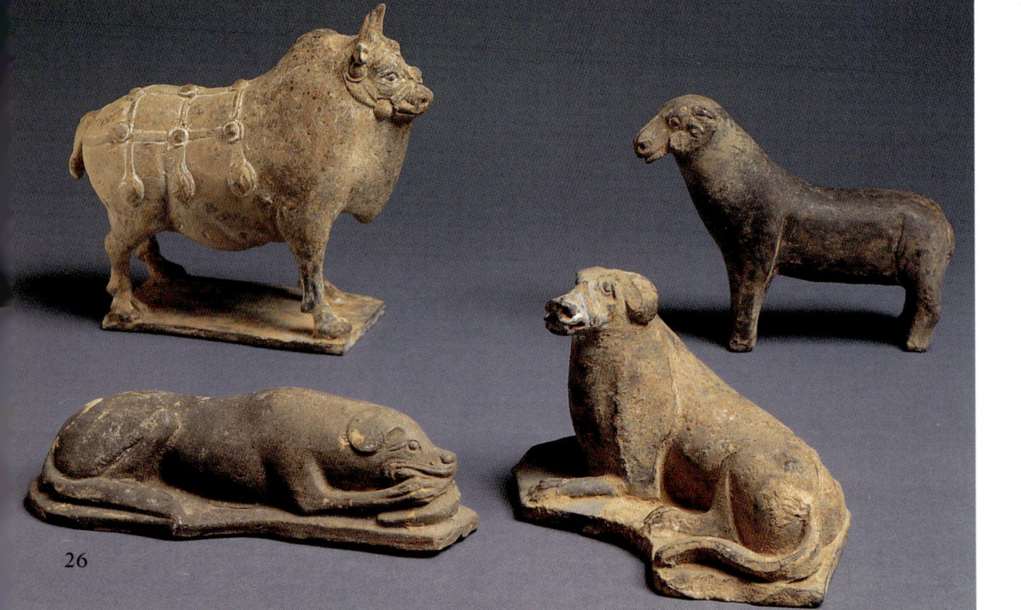

were also offered to the five tutelary spirits of the house: the porch, the doorway, the well, the stove, and the atrium pool. A time of rejoicing and renewal, the New Year celebration was marked by feasting with friends and exchange of wishes for long life and good health. Other important festivities were held at equinoxes and solstices, marked by purification rites, sacrificial offerings and family banquets. The Dragon Boat Festival, for example, was held at the summer solstice (June 21) and celebrated the transplantation of young rice plants before the torrential summer rains. It was heralded by river parades, boat races and offerings of rice, through which the ancestors took all bad spirits back to the land of the dead. The Mid-Autumn Moon Festival was held around the time of the autumn equinox. It celebrated the successful reaping of the grain crops with women presenting food offerings in honor of the moon. These major celebrations are still observed in Chinese communities around the world today. [10]

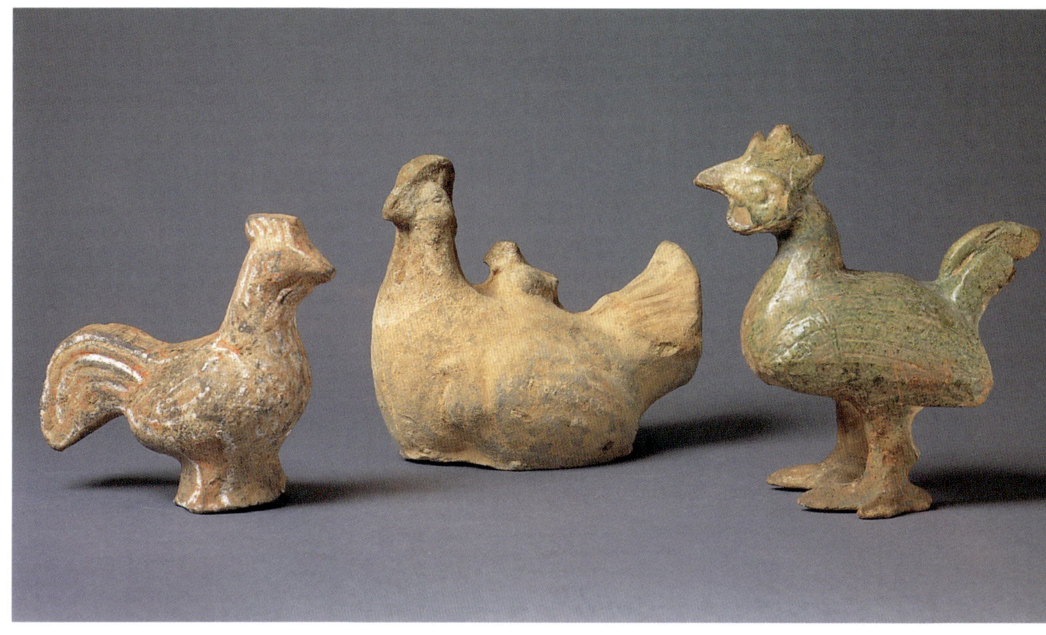

8.
ROOSTER
(OBJECT #29)
HEN WITH CHICK
(OBJECT #30)
ROOSTER
(OBJECT #31)

Many of the agricultural seasons and ancient rituals are documented by surviving Han texts such as the Simin yueling (Monthly Instructions for the Four Social Classes), a kind of family almanac which discusses silk production, medicine preparation, preservation of foodstuffs, social activities and family rites. It was written by Cui Shi (c. 110-170), who came from a family of Han Dynasty officials and landowners. During the latter Han period, a landowner served as a kind of local administrator, working the land of his estate alongside peasants and servants. The Simin yueling helped him plan production work, organize military training to fend off bandits, prepare for seasonal festivities, and offer charity to the poor. [11]

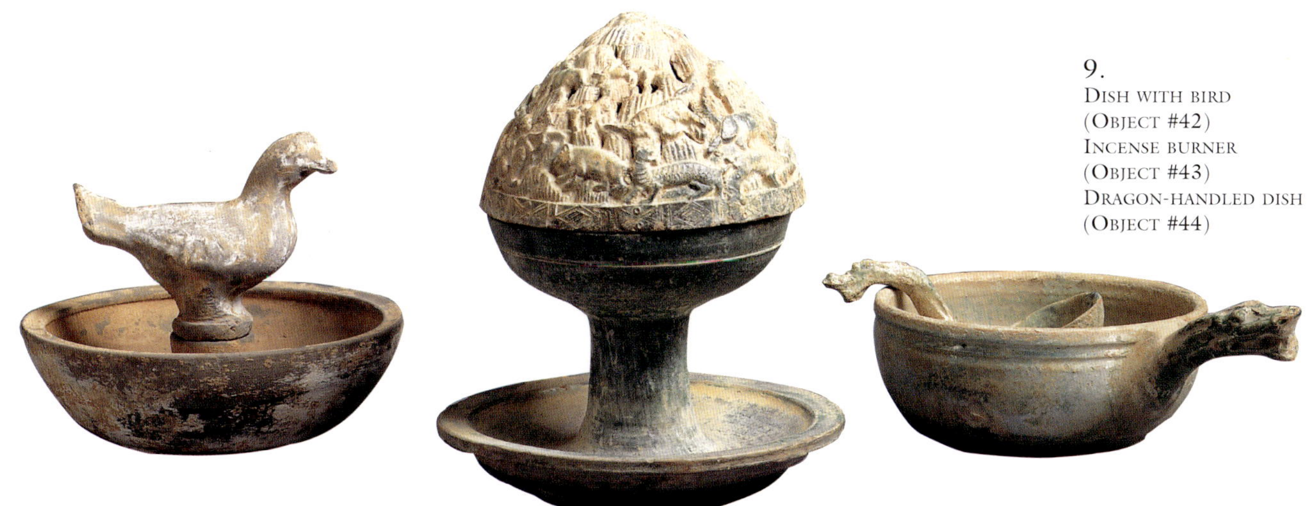

9.
DISH WITH BIRD
(OBJECT #42)
INCENSE BURNER
(OBJECT #43)
DRAGON-HANDLED DISH
(OBJECT #44)

While many of the *mingqi* clearly imitate the accoutrements of everyday life, others mirror a concern for the soul of the deceased on its journey into the netherworld. An example of this is a wellhead bearing relief designs of mythological creatures. (Figure 11) On the longer sides of the wellhead a dragon and tiger are depicted. The tiger is in combat with two superhumans and the dragon, preceded by a running figure, carries a small human figure on his back. This depiction is linked to the concept of the dual soul, consisting of the *hun* and the *po*, with the *hun* ascending to the realm of the immortals on the back of a dragon. Thus, this wellhead served a double function in the tomb: it provided a source of water for the deceased and also illustrated the soul's immortality. [12]

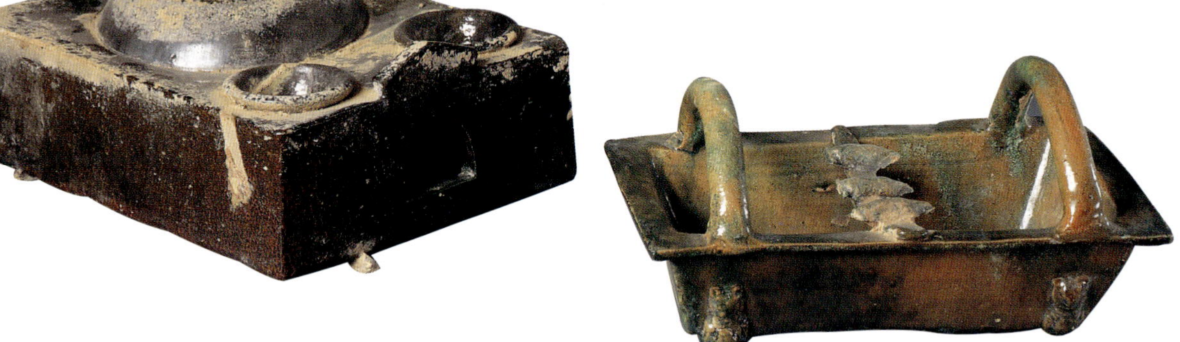

10.
Stove with chimney
(Object #40)
Cricket roaster
(Object #41)

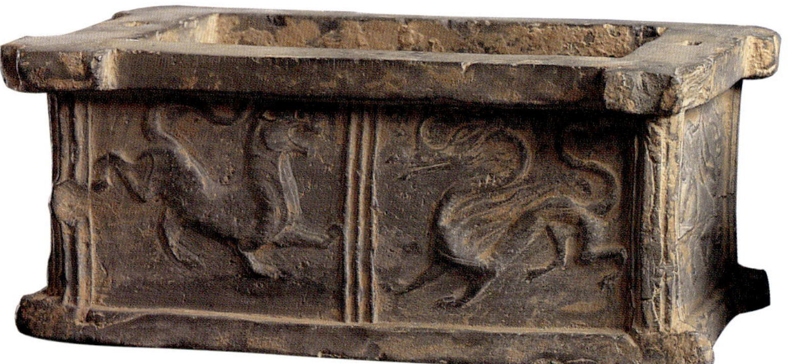

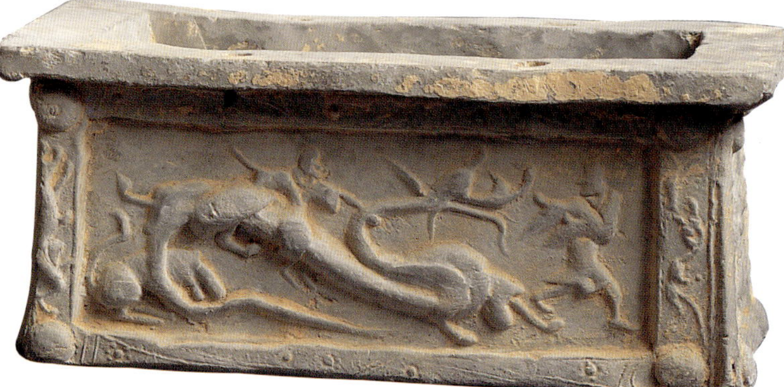

11.
Wellhead with animals of the four directions
(Object #19)
Wellhead with dragon and tiger relief designs
(Object #20)

NOTES:

1. Michele Pirazzoli-t'Serstevens, The Han Dynasty, pp. 92-97.

2. Candace J. Lewis, "Tall Towers of the Han," pp. 45-54.

3. Candace J. Lewis, Into the Afterlife: Han and Six Dynasties Chinese Tomb Sculpture from the Schloss Collection, p. 68.

4. Liang Ssu-ch'eng, A Pictorial History of Chinese Architecture (edited by Wilma Fairbank), pp. 9-21.

5. Candace J. Lewis, "Tall Towers of the Han," p. 47.

6. Robert Temple, The Genius of China, pp. 15-20.

7. Michele Pirazzoli-t'Serstevens, The Han Dynasty, pp. 65-70.

8. Janet Baker, Appeasing the Spirits, pp. 38-39.

9. Ka Bo Tsang, "Chinese Pig Tales," Archaeology, March/April 1996, pp. 52-57.

10. Carol Stepanchuk and Charles Wong, Mooncakes and Hungry Ghosts: Festivals of China, pp. 1-60, describes in great detail the rituals and beliefs of these three major festivals in both the past and the present.

11. Michele Pirazzoli-t'Serstevens, The Han Dynasty, pp. 175-179.

12. Candace J. Lewis, Into the Afterlife, p. 40.

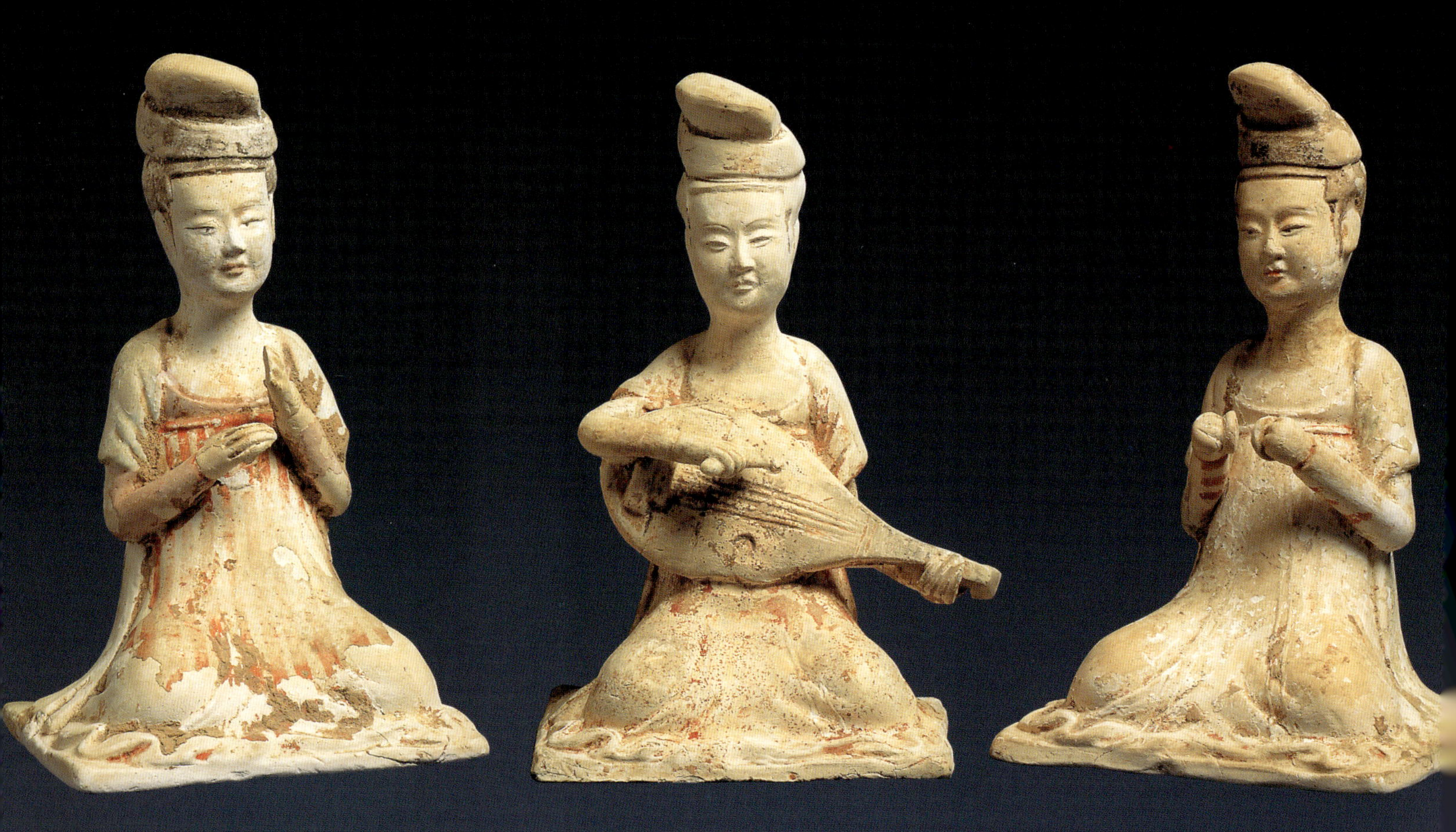

Trio of seated musicians (Object #83)

Social and Cultural Life

Mingqi reveal a great deal about ancient Chinese society. Some illustrate the division of social classes and an increasing ethnic diversity via their costumes and hairstyle, while others focus on entertainment such as music, dance and storytelling. While poetry, literature and histories refer to some of these cultural aspects of ancient Chinese life, few other visual records survive that offer such a graphic and detailed depiction of actual people who lived more than two thousand years ago.

During the Han Dynasty, representations of human figures constituted a small percent of *mingqi*. Standing figures of men and women clad in long robes worn over trousers show that their attire was distinguished only by decorative details and accessories denoting gender and class distinctions. Their overall uniformity reveals a preference for utilitarianism and simplicity in personal adornment. Women gathered their hair into a bun and preferred robes with wide hems and sleeves while men revealed their social status through a variety of headgear. Invariably, the figures of both sexes are shown with the hands clasped in a gesture of respect, reflecting Han society's emphasis on political and social unity (Figure 13). Recently discovered tomb sculpture of nude male and female figures originally wore fabric clothing. (Figure 12)

The Bowers Museum of Cultural Art
2002 N. MAIN STREET
SANTA ANA, CA 92706
(714) 567-3600
TR# : 0008103 11/09/96
MBR#: *** NOT ON FILE
***
ITEM # DESCRIPTION PRICE QTY AMOUNT
996554 SEEKING IMMORTALITY CATALOG 24.95 1 24.95
24.95
NET TRANS:
LESS DISCOUNT: .00
FREIGHT: .00
SALES TAX: 1.93

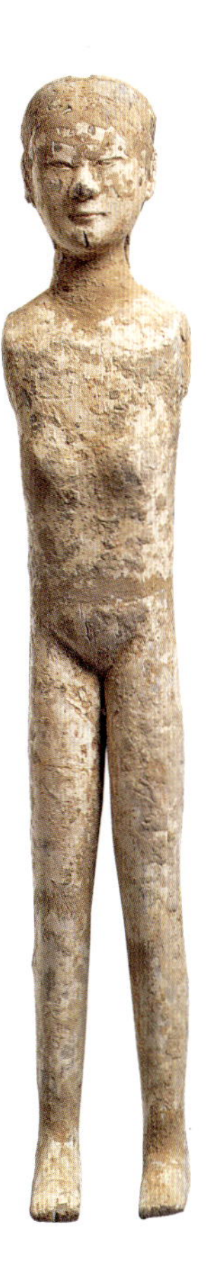
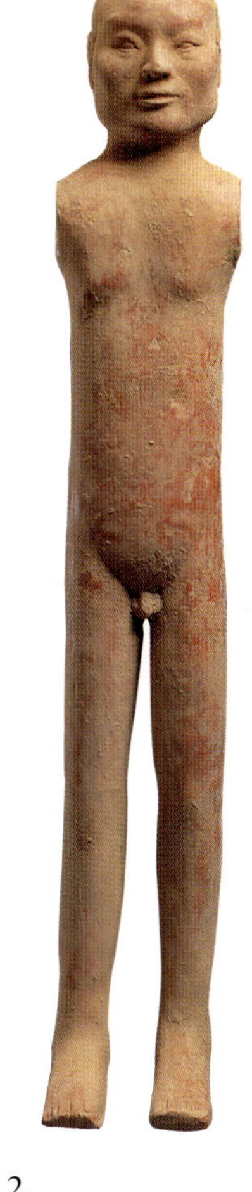

12.
TWO NUDE FIGURES
(OBJECT #49)

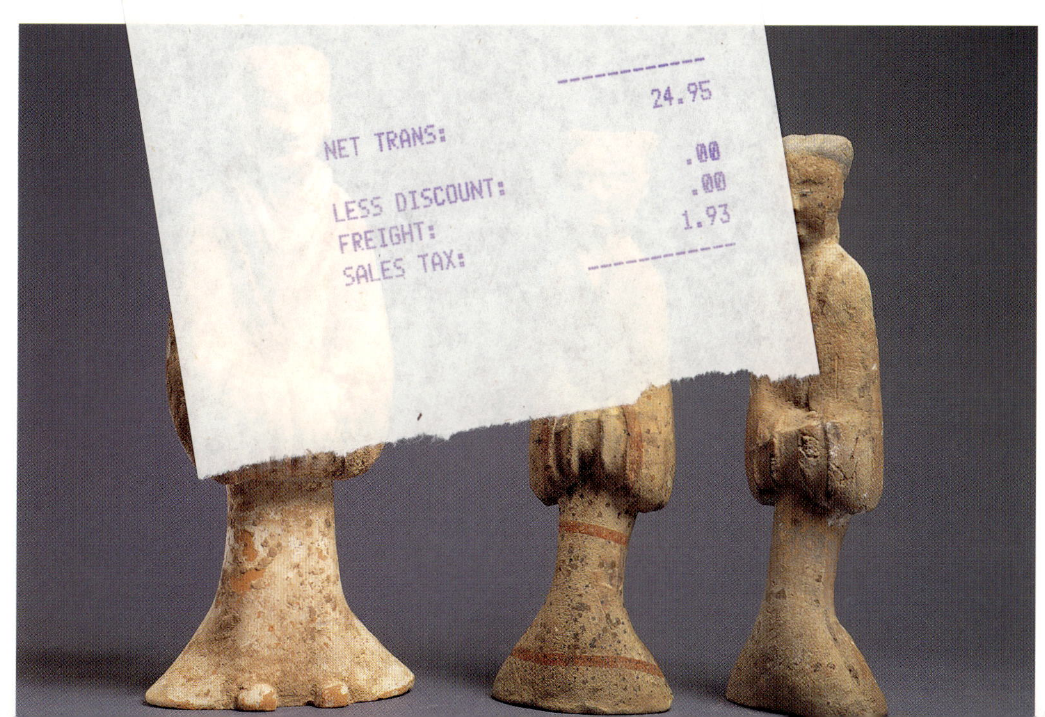

13.
GENTLEMAN
(OBJECT #52)
PAIR OF LADIES
(OBJECT #53)

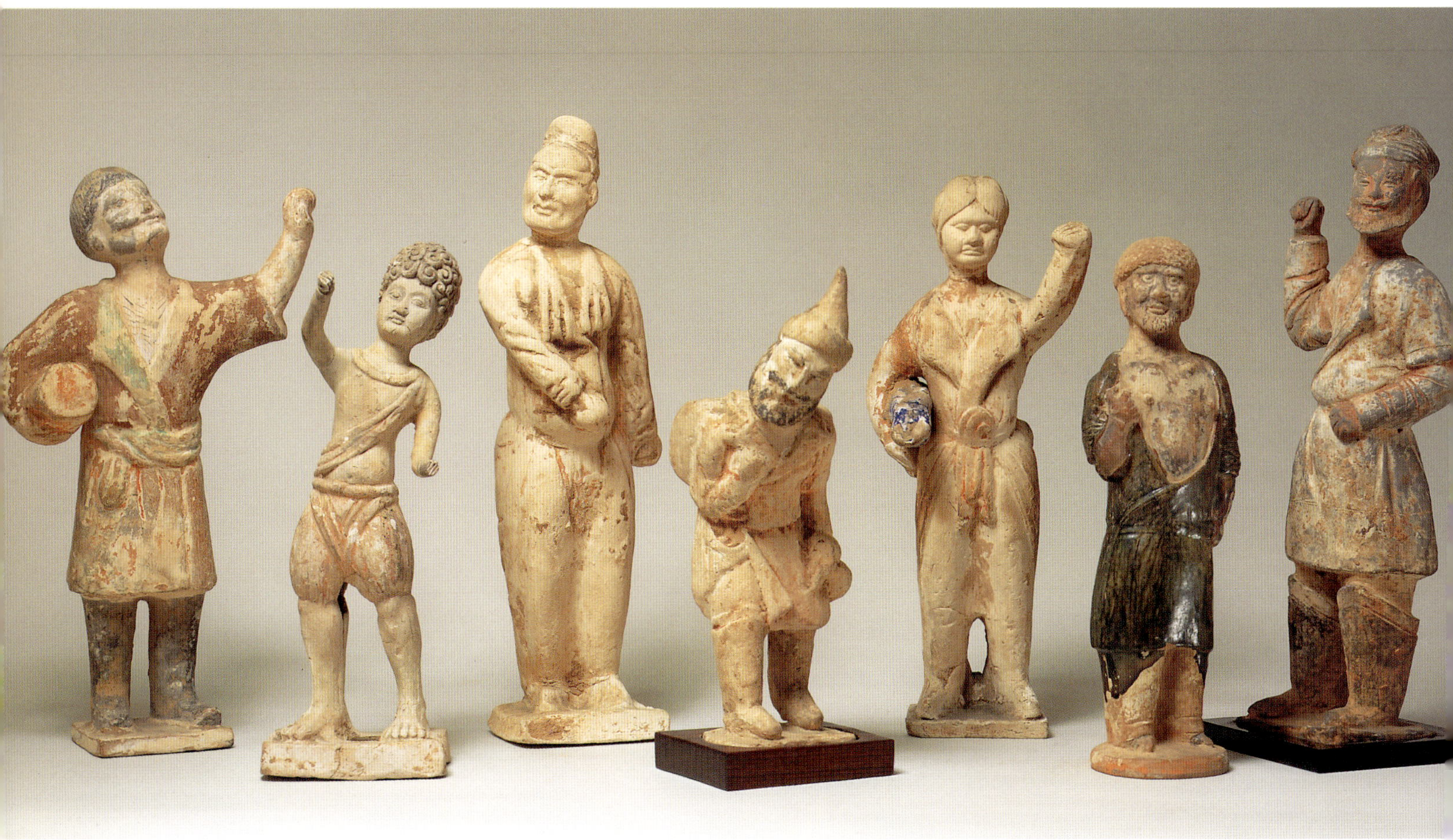

14.
Seven foreign men
(Object #88)

The political and social turmoil brought about by the downfall of the Han empire and the resulting conflicts between warring factions during the Six Dynasties period is reflected in a greater ethnic diversity among *mingqi*. As nomadic tribes roamed the border regions and Buddhist pilgrims travelled the Silk Route, Chinese society became receptive to new influences. Many non-Chinese peoples entered the country as military captives or as refugees from persecution in their native land. These immigrants comprised a new class of workers who were frequently employed as servants, grooms, entertainers or even court officials.[2] This diversity of ethnic types in *mingqi* begins to appear in the Six Dynasties and continues through the Sui and Tang periods. However, their facial features and costume details offer only limited clues as to their diverse places of origin.

While establishing contacts with a variety of foreigners, China had the closest relations with the multitude of Turkic tribes to the northwest. These particular alliances were necessary to secure peace and a domination of Central Asia and the Silk Route. Male *mingqi* distinguished by long noses, mustaches, dark eyebrows and round eyes as well as their native costumes of belted tunics, baggy trousers tucked into boots, hats and capes chronicle this novel influx of foreign merchants, servants and attendants. During the Tang Dynasty, foreigners from as far abroad as India and the Near East are realistically depicted with bare torsos, muscular physiques, curly hair and exotic jewelry. (Figure 14)

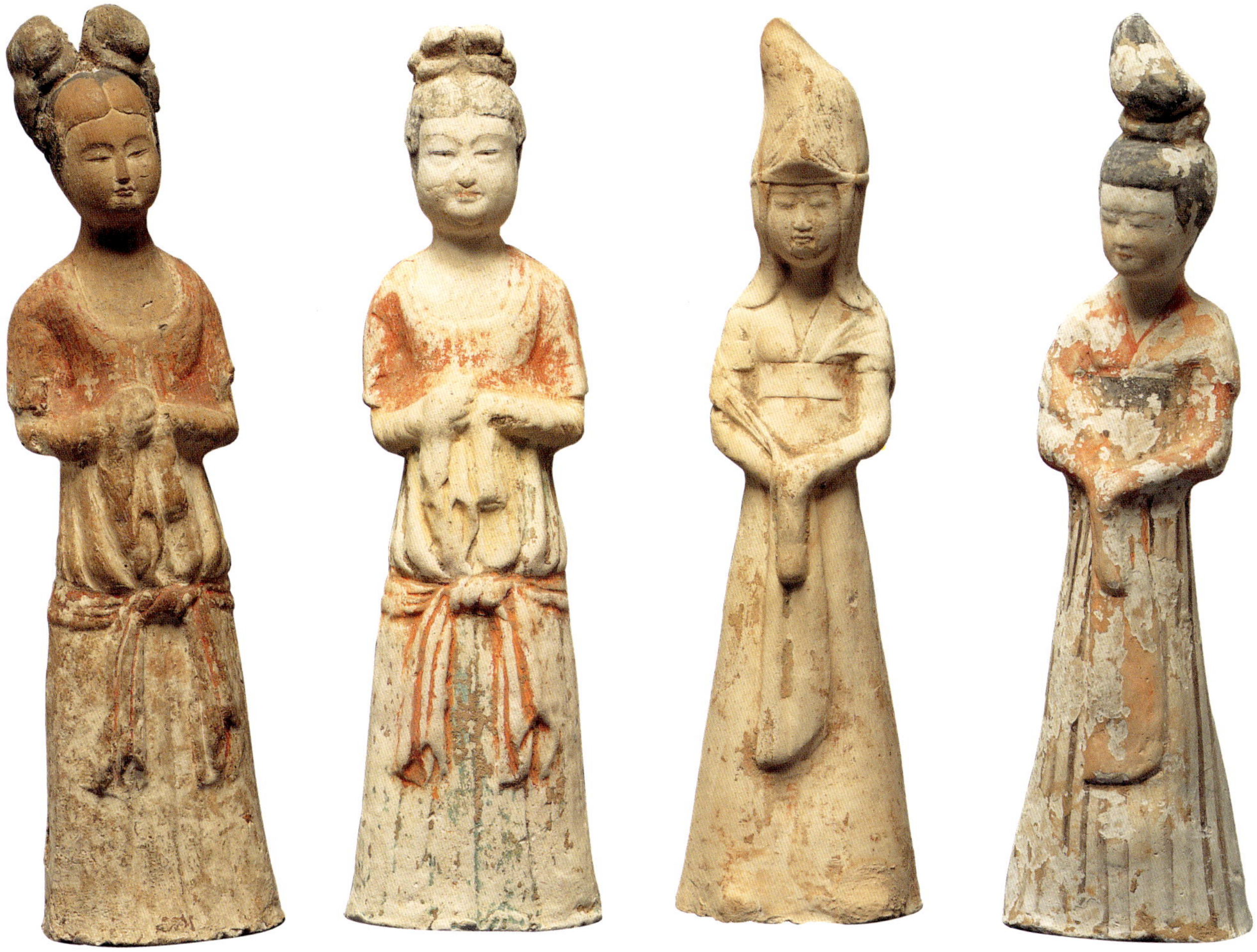

15.
Four court ladies
(Object #85)

While the presence of foreign women was limited, Chinese women enthusiastically adopted foreign dress and fashion. In the Six Dynasties period, the reserved elegance of the long robe gives way to more voluminous skirts falling from close-fitting high-waisted bodices accented by fluttering ribbons. [3] By the Sui and early Tang, feminine attire blossoms into a display of styles brought directly from Central Asia and Persia. A low-cut chemise-style dress with flaring skirt, sometimes with a sash tied below the hips, accompanied by a short-sleeved jacket and a stole draped over the shoulders was particularly popular. [4] (Figure 15) These new fashions were frequently made from fabrics with brocaded or embroidered designs in floral or geometric patterns. Examples of such fabrics showing Middle Eastern motifs such as medallions enclosing lions or griffins, have been excavated from seventh century tombs along the Silk Route.[5] (Figure 16) Upswept hairstyles of single or double topknots and a variety of headgear, including tiaras, hoods, and even helmets enhanced the fashionable ensembles. [6]

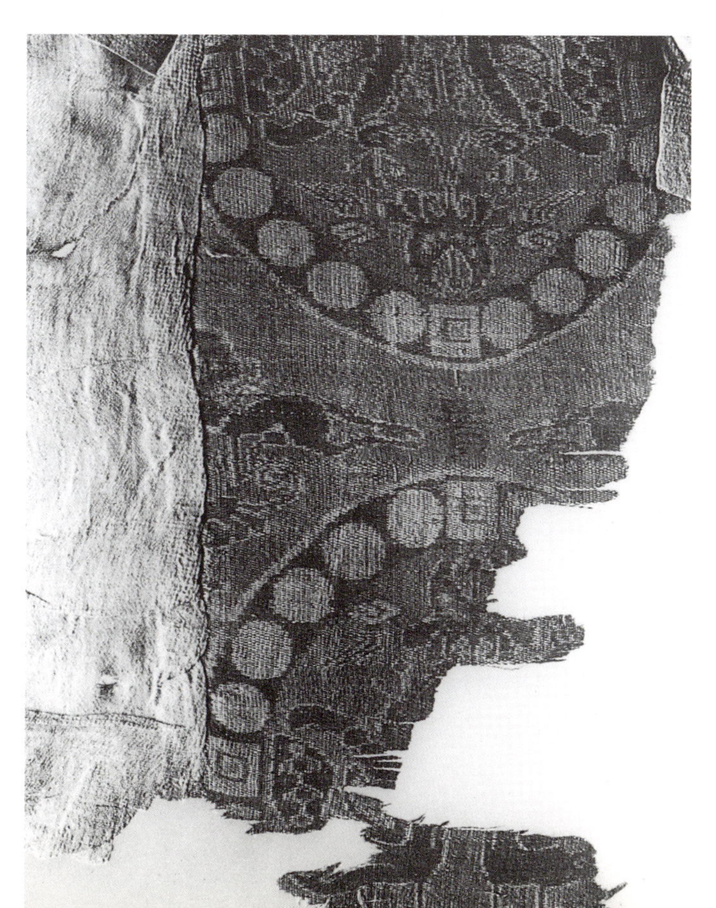

16.
Tang Dynasty textile fragment excavated from Astana tombs. Turfan, Xinjiang province
From Sichou Zhilu: Han Tang Zhiwu, (1973).

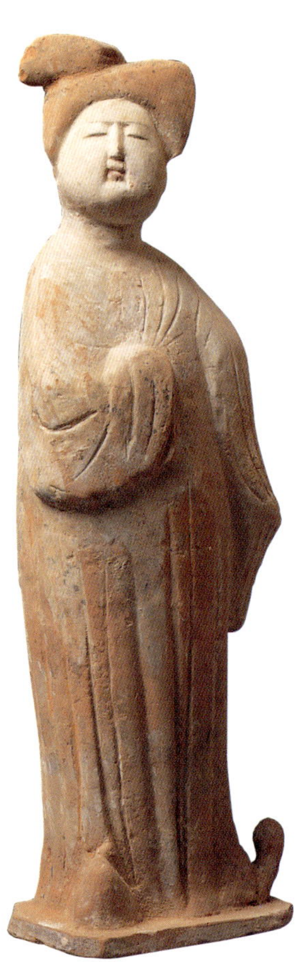
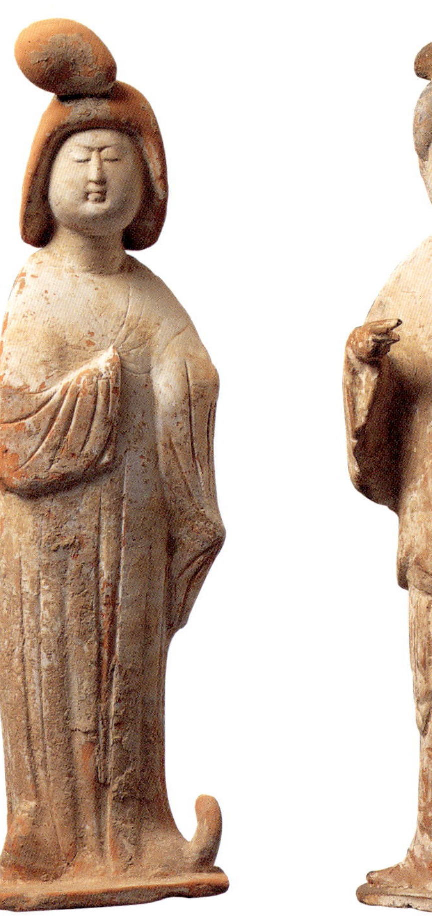
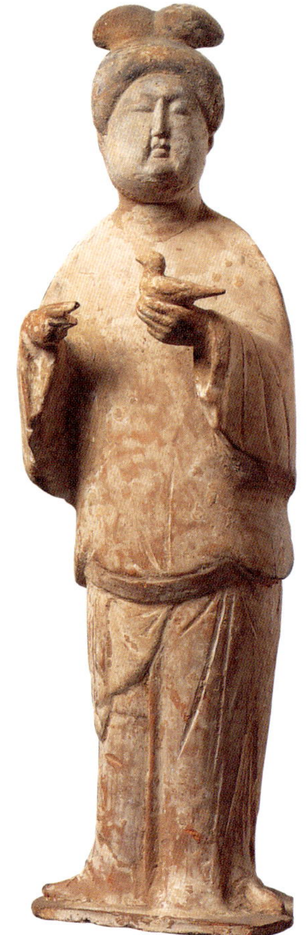
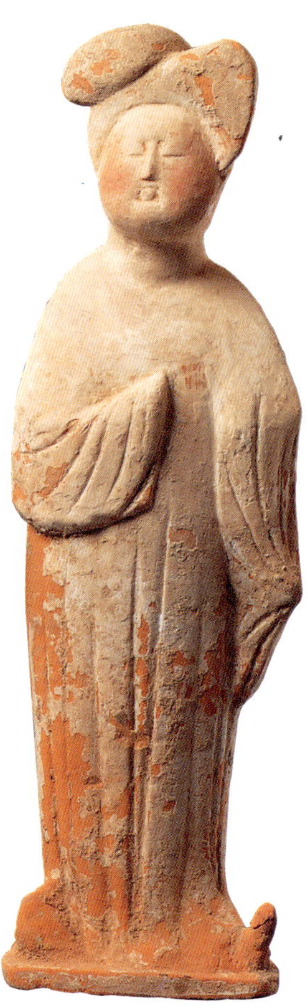

17.
FOUR COURT LADIES
(OBJECTS #87)

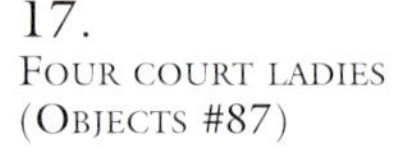

While court officials and high-ranking ladies still wore the traditional Chinese-style robes for ceremonial occasions, the foreign styles became the rage of Chang'an, especially among the upper classes. By the early seventh century the variety of styles and fashions had become complex enough for the Emperor to set forth official codes specifying costumes, hats and even vehicles appropriate for each social rank, from the Emperor down to the lowest petty officials. [7] In the eighth century, the preference for tight-fitting foreign fashions adorning a slender female form was gradually replaced by one for voluptuous women dressed in loose, gauzy gowns. This aesthetic change was embodied by the favorite concubine of the Tang emperor Minghuang, Yang Guifei, whose ample physique was legendary and is reflected in later Tang *mingqi* "fat ladies" whose matronly countenances offer a marked contrast to the girlish figures and delicate faces of Sui and early Tang ladies. [8] (Figure 17)

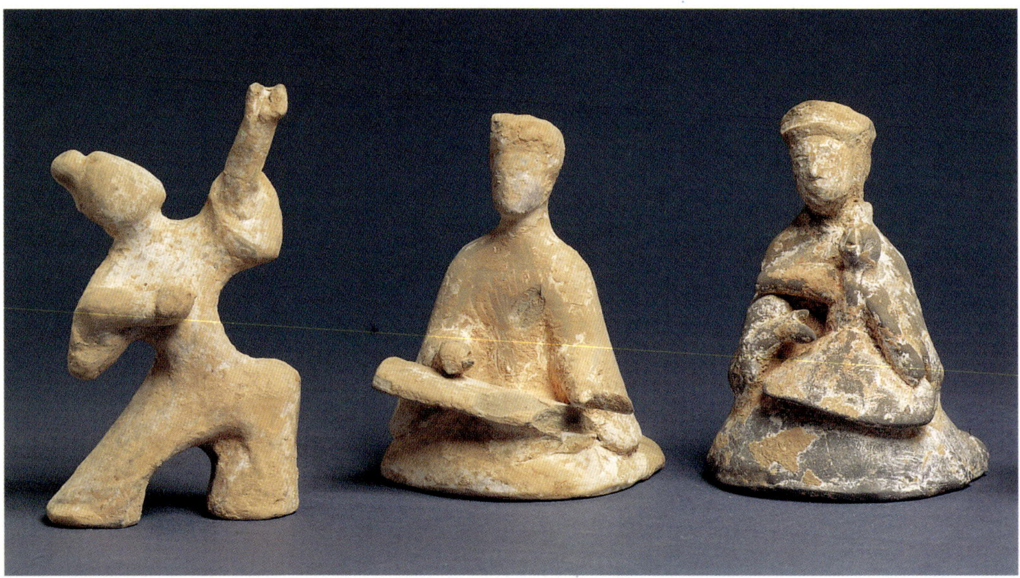

18.
DANCER
(OBJECT #54)
SEATED ZITHER PLAYER
(OBJECT #55)
SEATED MOTHER AND CHILD
(OBJECT #56)

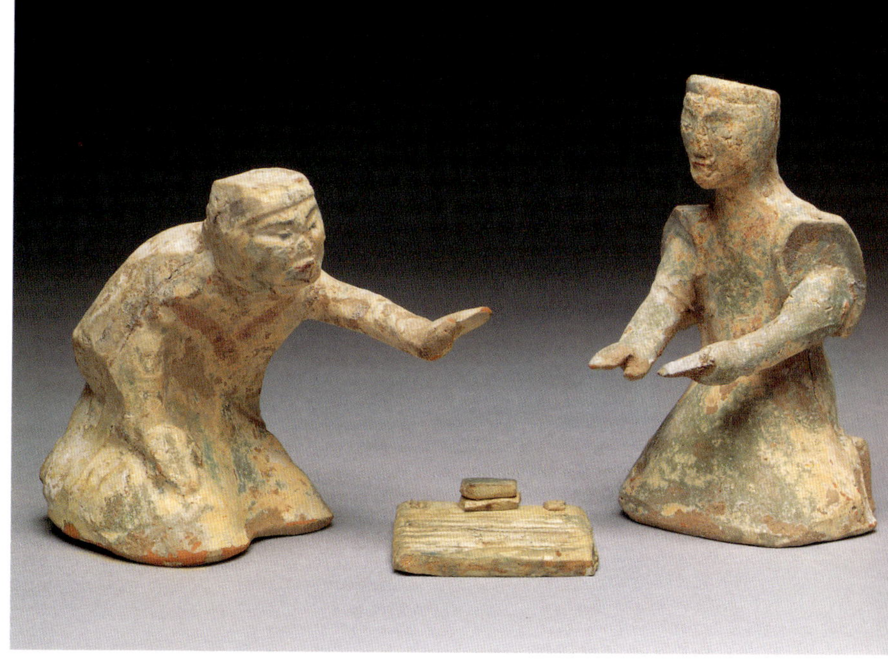

19.
LIUBO PLAYERS
(OBJECT #60)

The distinction between formal or Chinese style and informal or foreign style also extended into the realm of entertainment. *Mingqi* include figures of storytellers, jugglers, *liubo* (chess) players, musicians and dancers. (Figure 18) Historical records and mural paintings in numerous tombs confirm that some of these pursuits were part of everyday life as well as a component of elaborate funerary feasts for the deceased. [9] Images of *liubo* players painted in tombs suggest that the immortals also played this game in their celestial realm. The square board represented the earth, while the black and white pieces represented the *yin* and *yang* of the heavenly bodies of the cosmos. [10] (Figure 19) Among Han *mingqi*, figures of storytellers and jugglers are characterized by dramatic or comic poses, gestures and a lively sense of action. Bordering on the grotesque, these storytellers who sang and acted out their stories to the beat of their own drums were part of circus-like performances offered in the palaces of the elite and the residences of officials and some commoners. (Figure 20)

Dance and music characterized by many stylistic influences and changes dominated Chinese cultural life from the Han through the Tang Dynasties. In the Han Dynasty, ritual or ceremonial music played on stone chimes, bells and zithers was used to further self-cultivation and community harmony. Ceremonial texts of the time describe the music of a well-governed state as upright, orderly and not overly stimulating. Yet, music and dance were also part of festive gatherings that featured acrobats, wrestlers, tightrope walkers, exotic animals and plentiful food. Han texts indicate that many such entertain-

20.
DANCER
(OBJECT #61)
BRICK WITH RELIEF DEPICTING JUGGLER
(OBJECT #62)

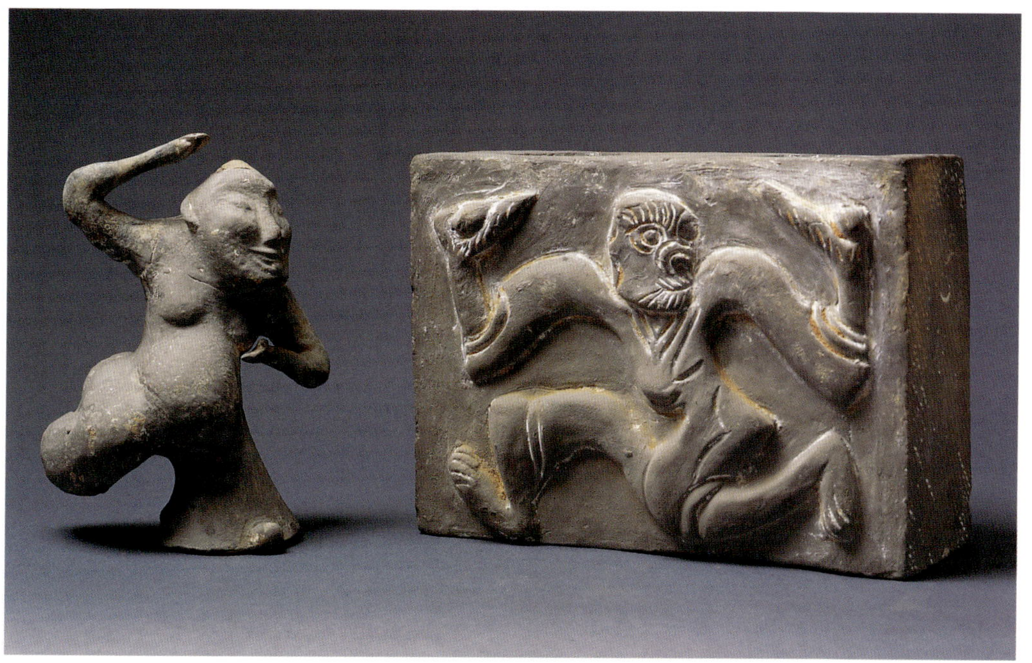

ers were probably trained slaves, sometimes of non-Chinese ethnicity. Their performances injected an element of the unorthodox or exotic into the austerity and conventionality of the prescribed ritual performances. [11]

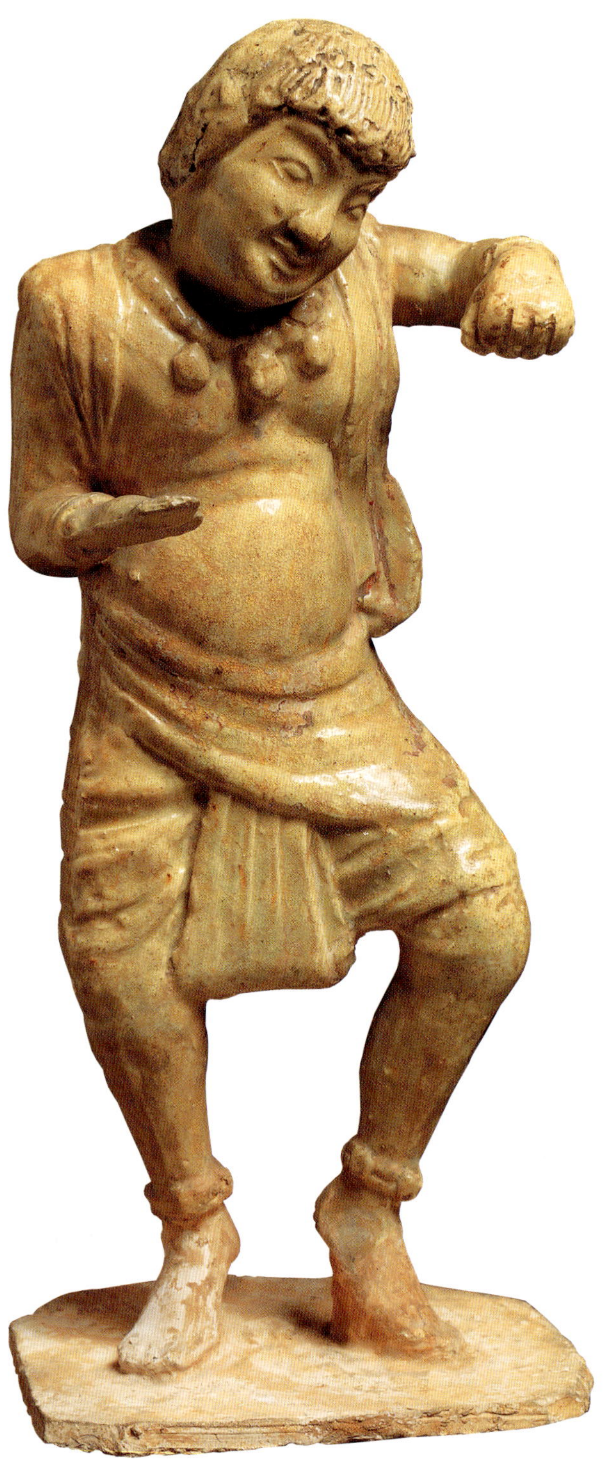

21.
Foreign dancer
(Object #84)

By the Sui and Tang Dynasties, foreign musicians were incorporated into the ranks of court employees to perform at "informal" palace entertainments, while "formal" ceremonies still required traditional Chinese music dating back to the Han Dynasty. Many instruments still played in China today such as the lute, oboe, flute, cymbals and clappers were adopted at that time from cultures traversing the Silk Route. Ensembles of female musicians appear among *mingqi* more frequently than male musicians while dancers of either gender, especially foreigners, seem to have been extremely popular. Poets of the Tang described some of these dances as having whirling movements "like snowflakes or leaves dancing in the air." [12] Exotic forms of song and dance captivated the Chinese to such an extent that some, even the emperor, learned to perform "foreign" music themselves. (Figure 21)

Murals and stone carvings at Buddhist cave chapel sites across China illustrate that musical ensembles were incorporated into the concept of a Buddhist paradise. During the sixth and seventh centuries, the ascetic practices and beliefs of Chinese Buddhism gave way to new schools of beliefs that emphasized the concept of the Western Paradise of Amitabha Buddha who would grant entrance into his heavenly realm to any true believer who called out his name. Depictions of the Western Paradise were modelled after life in the Tang imperial court, with jewelled palaces forming the backdrop for a host of dancers, singers, musicians and heavenly attendants flanking the serene figure of Amitabha Buddha. These visionary scenes also attest to the Tang emperors' adaptation of Buddhism to indigenous Chinese beliefs of filial piety and material comfort in both this life and the afterlife.[13] (Figure 22)

In the realms of poetry, prose and the visual arts, writers and painters recorded the marvels that came from abroad. From distant kingdoms came royal tribute gifts such as precious gems and metals, costly brocades and magic potions, rare birds and beasts; all are elaborately described by authors of the eighth and ninth centuries whose nostalgic imagination was likely given to exaggeration. The writings of medieval art critics in China are filled with discussions of the exotic themes chosen by famous Tang artists, many of whom were commanded by the emperor to record the appearances of the "barbarians" who had arrived at the court in their native costumes. A mural depicting such foreign envoys came to light in recent decades with the excavation of the Tang tomb of Li Xian, known as Prince Zhanghuai, the second son of Emperor Gaozong and Empress Wu Zetian. He and his wife were interred about 711 in the imperial cemetery outside Chang'an. A section of the tomb mural shows three foreign envoys meeting with three

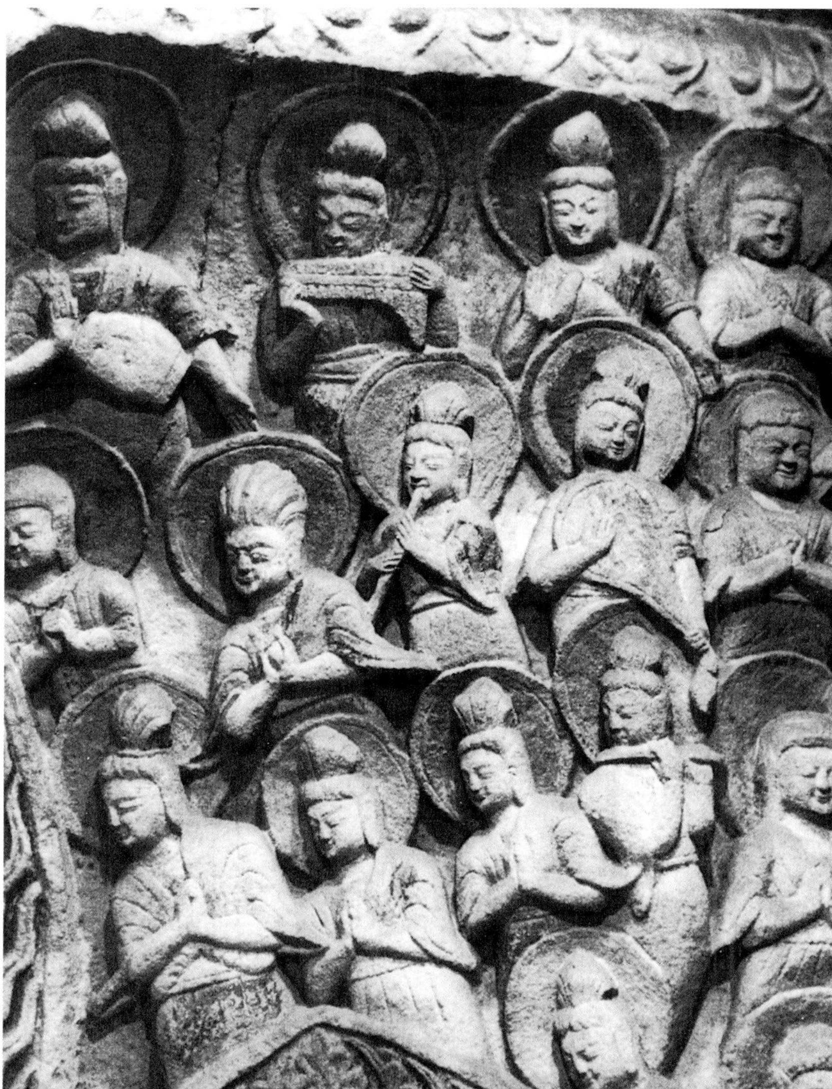

22.
Stone relief of heavenly musicians in Buddhist paradise at Yungang caves, fifth century. Datong, Shanxi province. From Yungang Shiku, (1977).

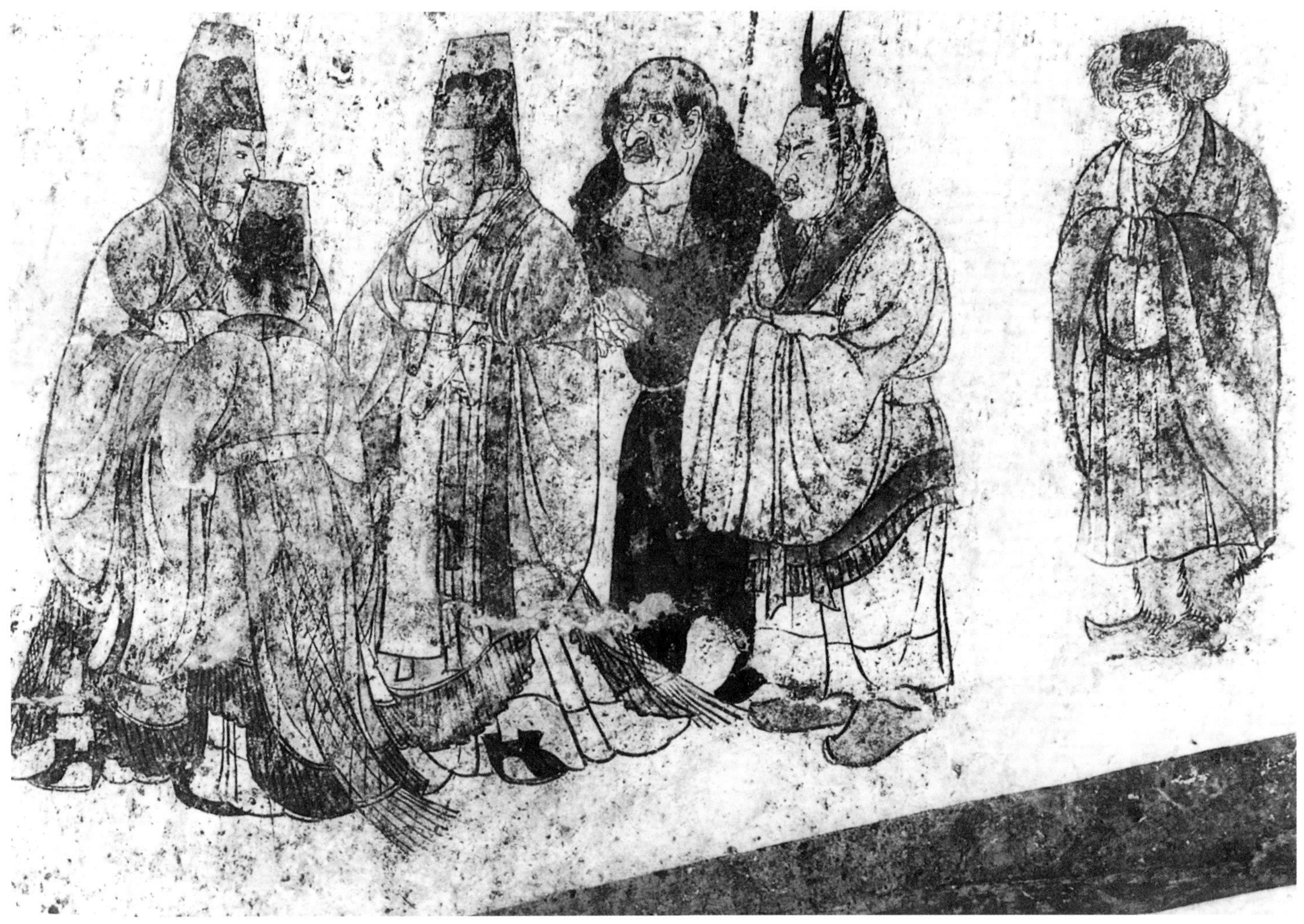

23.
Mural depicting foreigners offering tribute from the tomb of Li Xian, Prince Zhanghuai, early eighth century. Xian, Shaanxi province. From Tang Li Xian Mubihua, (1974).

Chinese mandarins. While the Chinese men at the left are dressed in court gowns, black gauze hats and sashes, the three envoys exhibit diverse costumes that reflect their different ethnic heritage. The man in a fur hat and pants at the far right may be from China's northeastern provinces, while the next figure is almost certainly Korean. He wears a robe that shows similarities to the Chinese costume, yet a cap which appears in murals found in Korean tombs. The third foreigner, a hawk-nosed, bald man, is of undetermined ethnic origin. The precision and attention to detail with which these exotic figures are portrayed suggests that the artist was familiar with many kinds of visitors to the Chinese capital. [14] (Figure 25)

While painting was traditionally elevated to a higher artistic status than sculpture, their close resemblance can be observed by a comparison between the murals painted in the very tombs where *mingqi* have been excavated. Mural paintings and tomb sculpture both portray the same people, activities and fashions, thus constituting a related body of dated evidence all the more noteworthy in light of the scant surviving examples of scroll paintings and wooden sculpture from the Han and Tang eras. [15]

NOTES:

1. Zhou Xun and Gao Chunming, 5000 Years of Chinese Costumes, pp. 32-33.

2. Edward H. Schafer, The Golden Peaches of Samarkand: A Study of T'ang Exotics, pp. 40-50.

3. 5000 Years of Chinese Costumes, pp. 54-55.

4. Ibid., pp. 76-77.

5. Xinjiang Weiwu'er Zizhiqu Bowuguan, Sichou Zhilu: Han Tang Zhiwu (The Silk Route: Han and Tang Textiles), plates 27-36.

6. Ezekiel Schloss, Ancient Chinese Ceramic Sculpture From Han to T'ang, pp. 150-157. See also Sunji, "Tangdai Funude Fuzhuang yu Huazhuang" ("Costume and Makeup of Tang Dynasty and Women"), Wenwu, 1984, #4, pp. 57-69.

7. 5000 Years of Chinese Costumes, pp. 76-77.

8. Ibid., p. 94.

9. Kenneth J. DeWoskin, "Music and Voices From the Han Tombs," Stories From China's Past, pp. 64-71.

10. Wu Hung, "Myths and Legends in Han Funerary Art," Stories from China's Past, pp. 77-77. See also, Robert Temple, The Genius of China, pp. 99-101.

11. Ibid., pp. 64-71.

12. Bai Juyi, "Swaying Dancers From Central Asia" (*huxuannu*) Bai Juyi: Two Hundred Selected Poems (trans. Rewi Alley).

13. Kenneth Ch'en, Buddhism in China, pp. 165-222.

14. Fontein and Wu, Han and T'ang Murals, pp. 90-94. See also Shaanxi Provincial Museum, Tangmu Bihua Zhenpin Xuancui (The Cream of Original Frescoes from Tang Tombs), pp. 40-41.

15. Han and T'ang Murals, pp. 9-16.

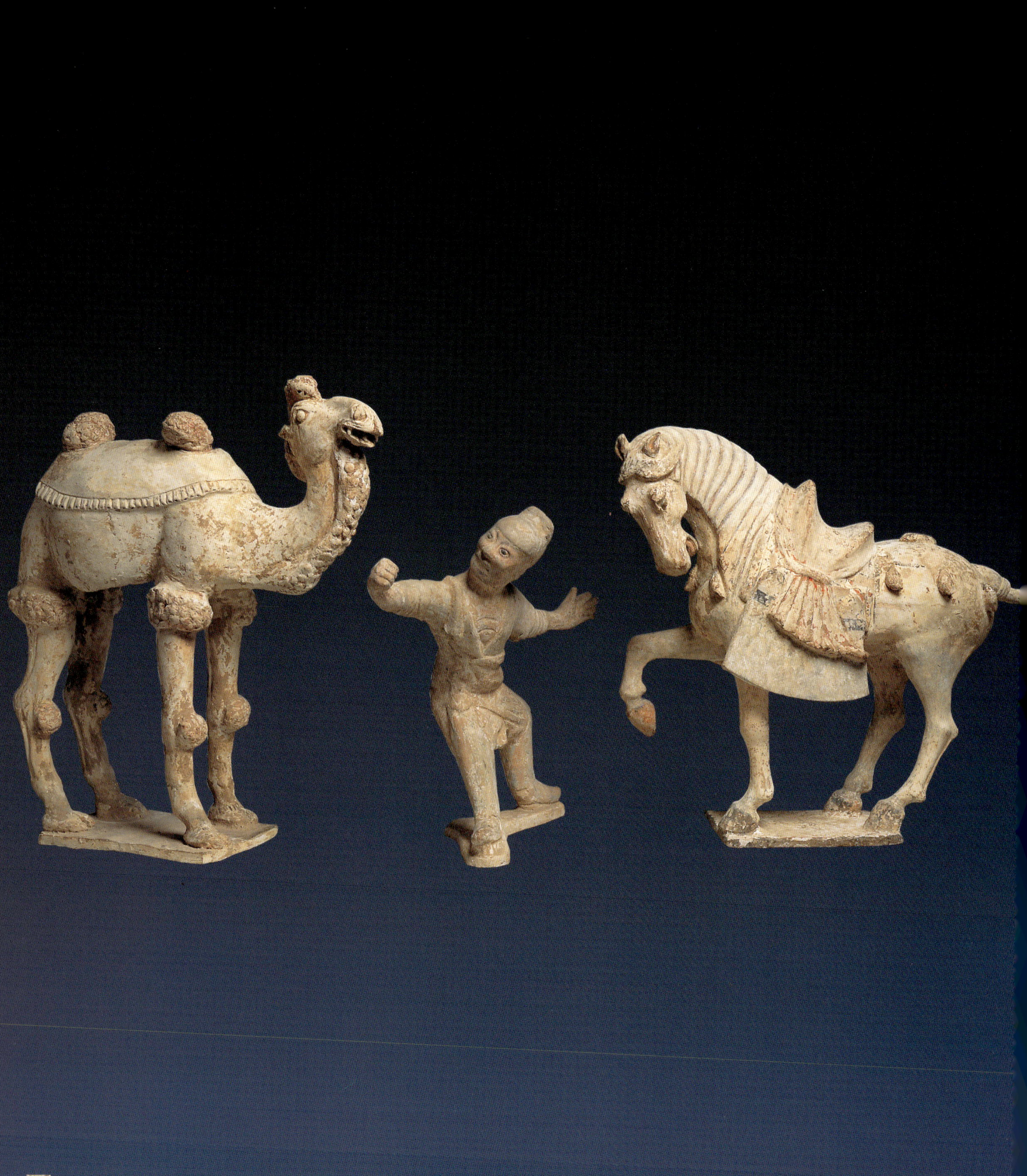

Military, Sport and Transportation

From tomb excavations predating the Han Dynasty, it is clear that the Chinese had developed elaborate carriages, vast armies, sophisticated weapons and, most importantly, adopted the art of horsemanship. Of all the animals both real and fantastic that appear in *mingqi*, the horse is the most significant in the study of transportation, sport and warfare in ancient China.

24.
POTTERY HORSE AND SOLDIER FROM THE PIT ACCOMPANYING THE TOMB OF QIN SHIHUANG, C. 210 BC. MUSEUM OF QIN FIGURES, LINTONG COUNTY, SHAANXI PROVINCE. FROM QIN SHIHUANG BINGMAYONG, (1992).

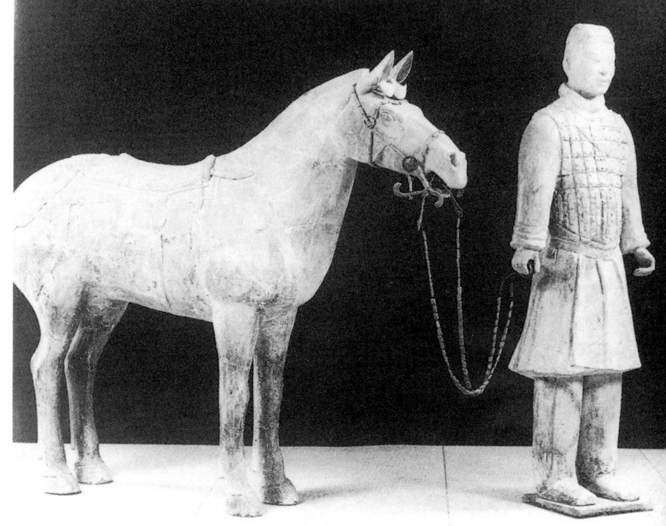

The excavation of the trenches auxiliary to the now famous tomb of the first Emperor Qin Shihuang (221 BC) brought to light thousands of lifesize terracotta solders, chariots and horses. The realistic detail of these sculptures allows differentiation of military ranks, including generals, calvary, infantry and archers (Figure 24). Many wear armor vests fashioned of small overlapping iron or leather plates to cover the entire torso, leaving the arms uncovered to allow freedom of movement. A similar form of armor is seen on Tang figures of warriors nearly a thousand years later, indicating its utility. Other figures wear additional armored shoulder guards. Under the armor Qin soldiers wore knee-length coats, tight-fitting pants and knee-high leather boots. Generals' armor was distinguished by the addition of decorative tassels on the shoulders and an official's cap worn over an elaborate chignon hairstyle. Originally painted in bright colors, these figures illuminate in great detail the varied aspects of early Chinese military life. [1]

The life-size *mingqi* soldiers were accompanied by full-size clay horses with plump torsos and sturdy legs. The horses were fitted with full harnesses including halter, mouthpiece, bridle and saddle; although lacking stirrups and martingale. The burial trenches included examples of bronze weapons, including the dagger-axe, spearhead, halberd, sword, crossbow and arrow. The arrowheads were designed for long-distance shooting, while the sword was used for close-range combat. All of the weapons found in Qin Shihuang's tomb display advanced technology in composing alloys, bronze casting and processing as well as standardization of types of weaponry.

FACING PAGE: BACTRIAN CAMEL (OBJECT #125), GROOM (OBJECT #126), PRANCING HORSE (OBJECT #127)

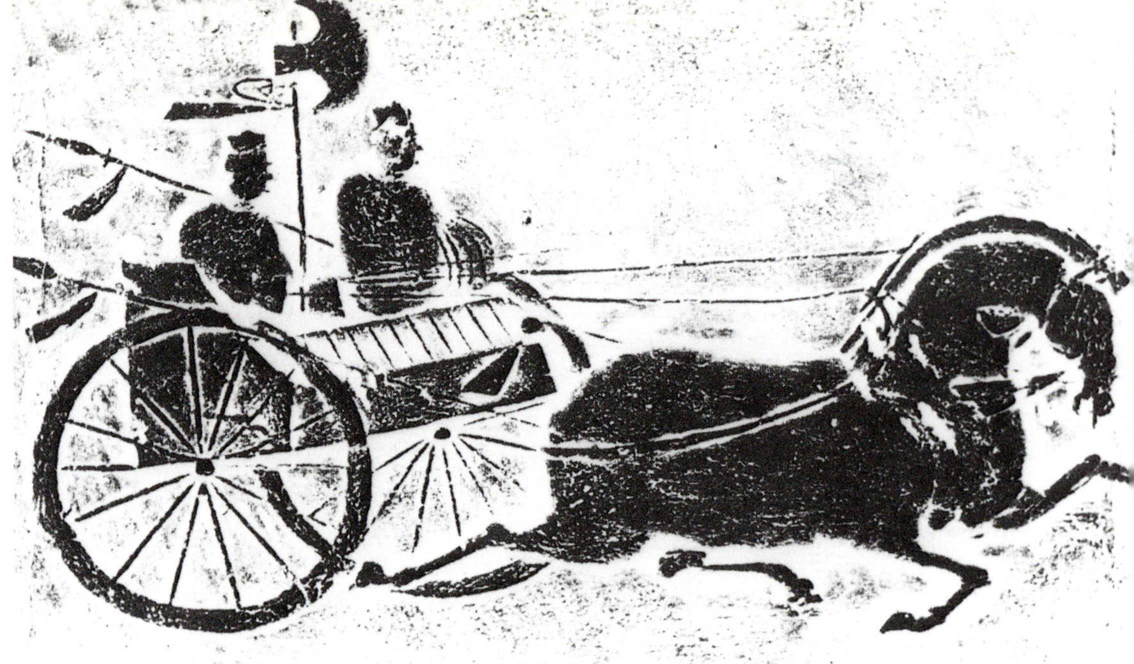

25.
Rubbing of tomb tile relief showing an "axe carriage"of the Han Dynasty. Sichuan Provincial Museum, Chengdu, Sichuan province. From Sichuan Handai Huaxiangzhuan Yu Handai Shehui, (1983).

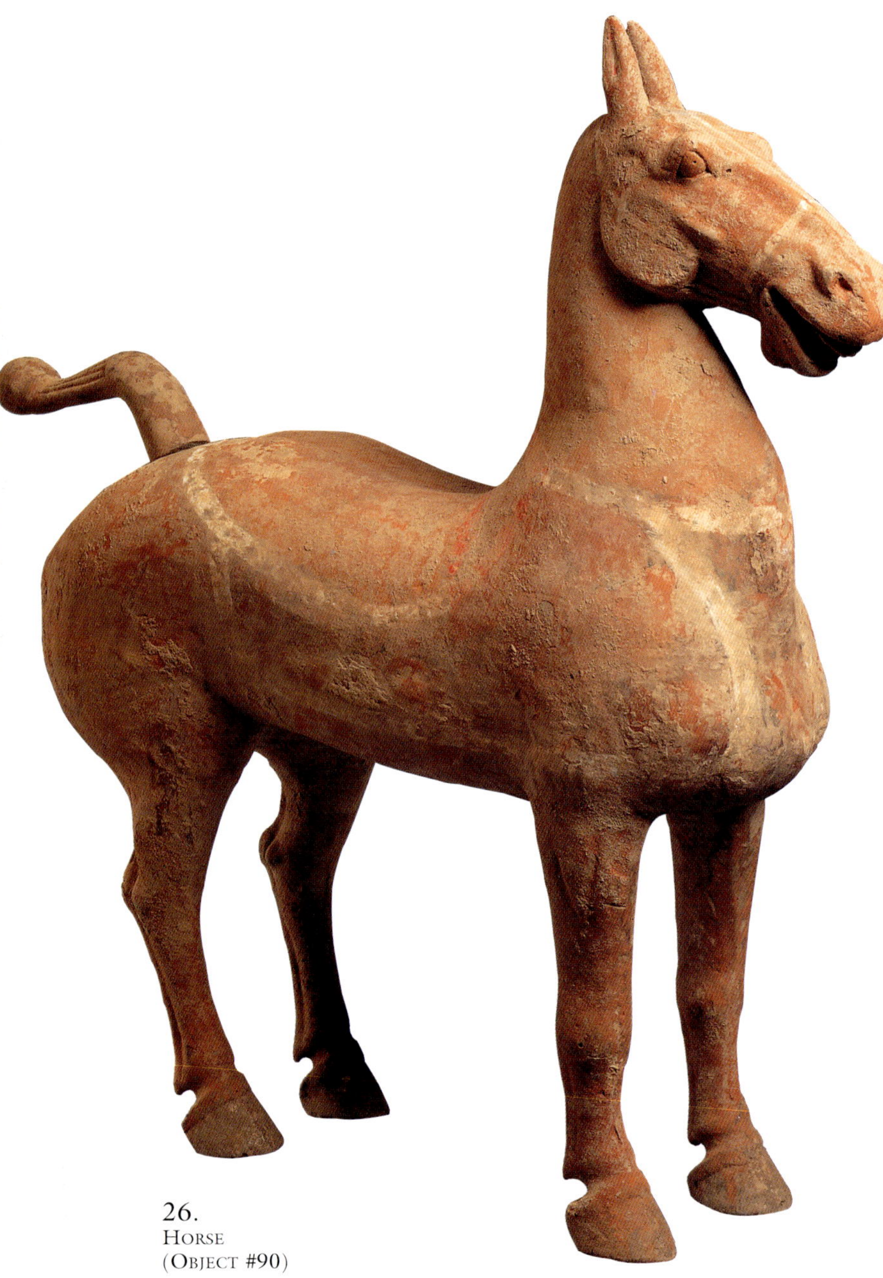

26.
Horse
(Object #90)

All that remained of the real wooden chariots in the Qin Emperor's burial was their imprint in the earth and some bronze trappings. Yet it is possible to reconstruct from this evidence a light-bodied two-wheeled square vehicle surrounded by a balustrade and drawn by four horses, two inside the yoke and two outside. The chariot carried a driver and one or two armored soldiers and was defended by infantrymen and sometimes cavalrymen. [2] During the Han period, the employment of cavalry eclipsed the use of chariots in the military, since chariots could only be utilized on flat, open terrain.

However, the use of chariots as a means of transportation for the social elite rose in popularity. According to the *Hou Han Shu* (History of the Later Han), a complicated carriage system took shape, in which the form of the carriage and the scale of a procession, including the number of horsemen, ushers, guards and other members of the retinue, indicated rank. Illustrations in some Han period tombs indicate that a variety of carriages, some open and some closed, were used. Some types, such as the open-air "axe carriage", were reserved exclusively for high-ranking officials, while others, such as the discreetly covered "canopy carriage", were used by aristocratic women. [3] (Figure 25)

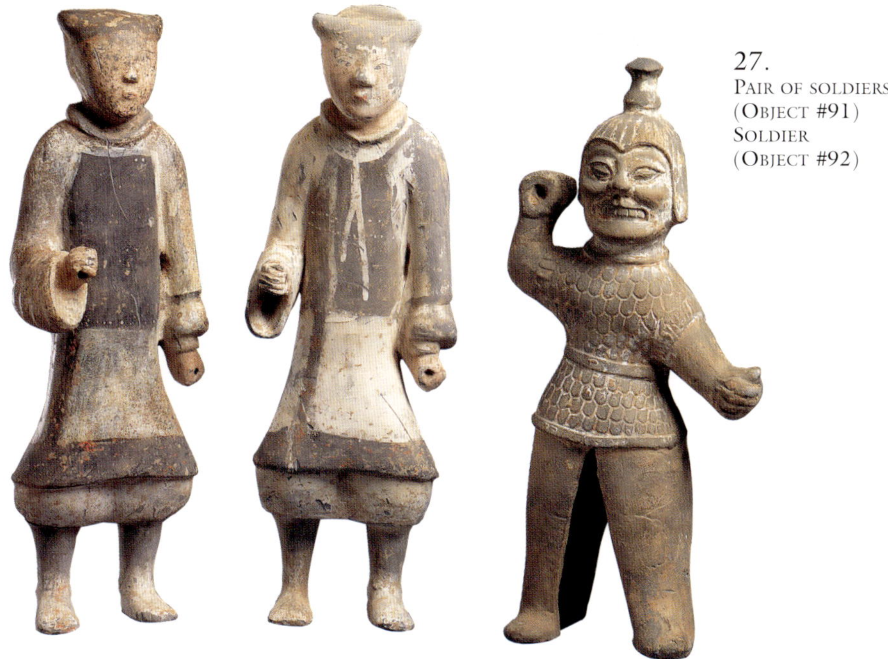

27.
Pair of soldiers
(Object #91)
Soldier
(Object #92)

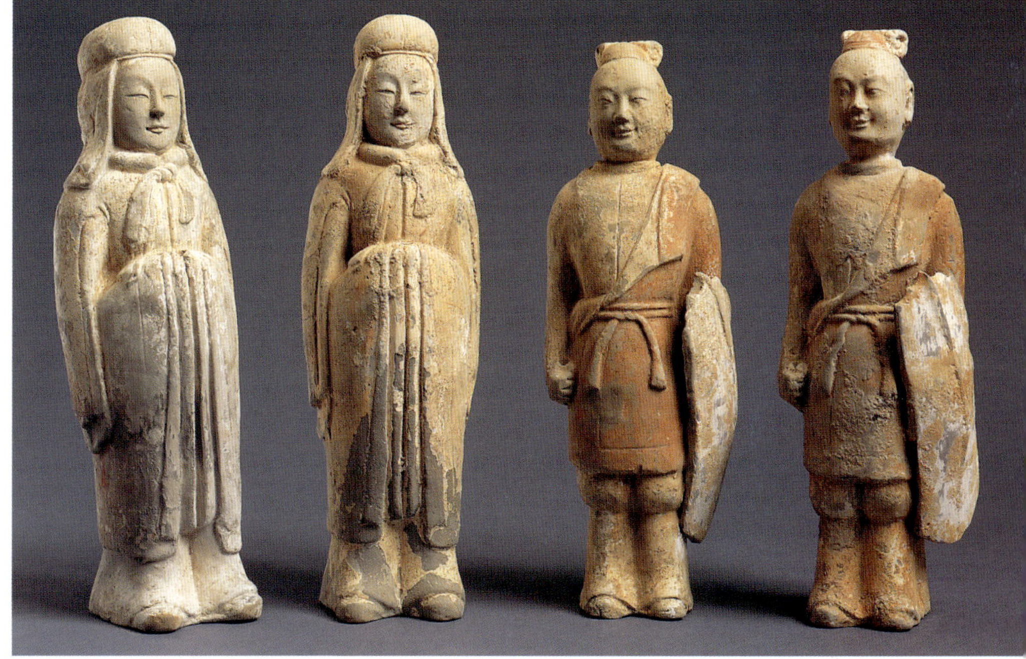

28.
Pair of officials
(Object #93)
Pair of soldiers with shields
(Object #94)

In the Qin army, draught and riding horses were both of the same stock, distinguished by a thick-set body and short legs. (Figure 26) However, horses found in Han period tombs testify to the fact that the Han emperors had acquired horses from the regions to the west of China. While the short legs of the Mongolian pony and Chinese domestic horse made them suitable as carriage and pack animals, the Han nobility sought to acquire the long-legged "heavenly horses" that came from the present-day area of Ferghana. These horses allowed victory in battles against the proto-Mongol Xiongnu warriors who threatened China's empire from the north. According to the *Han Shu* (History of the Han), in 177 BC the Emperor sent eighty-five thousand cavalrymen against the Xiongnu, and in 166 BC a thousand chariots and a hundred thousand cavalrymen defeated the Xiongnu in an attack near the capital at Changan. The use of such a number of cavalry in a single attack was unprecedented. In addition to the heavenly horses from Ferghana, the Chinese also prized the Samanthian horses from present-day Xinjiang province. The Samanthians were characterized by their massive bodies and shorter, sturdier legs that made them well suited for use in the cavalry. By the third century or so, Chinese warriors had also adopted the stirrup from the nomads of Central Asia and made widespread use of the crossbow, giving them a greater advantage in combat. [4] Musicians on horseback were also part of the Han military. Tomb illustrations show high-stepping horses striding in formation to the rhythm of bells, pipes, horns, drums, mouth organ and panpipes. Such instruments were undoubtedly used to send signals among the troops. [5] By the Six Dynasties period, examples of equestrian musicians appear in *mingqi* as well.

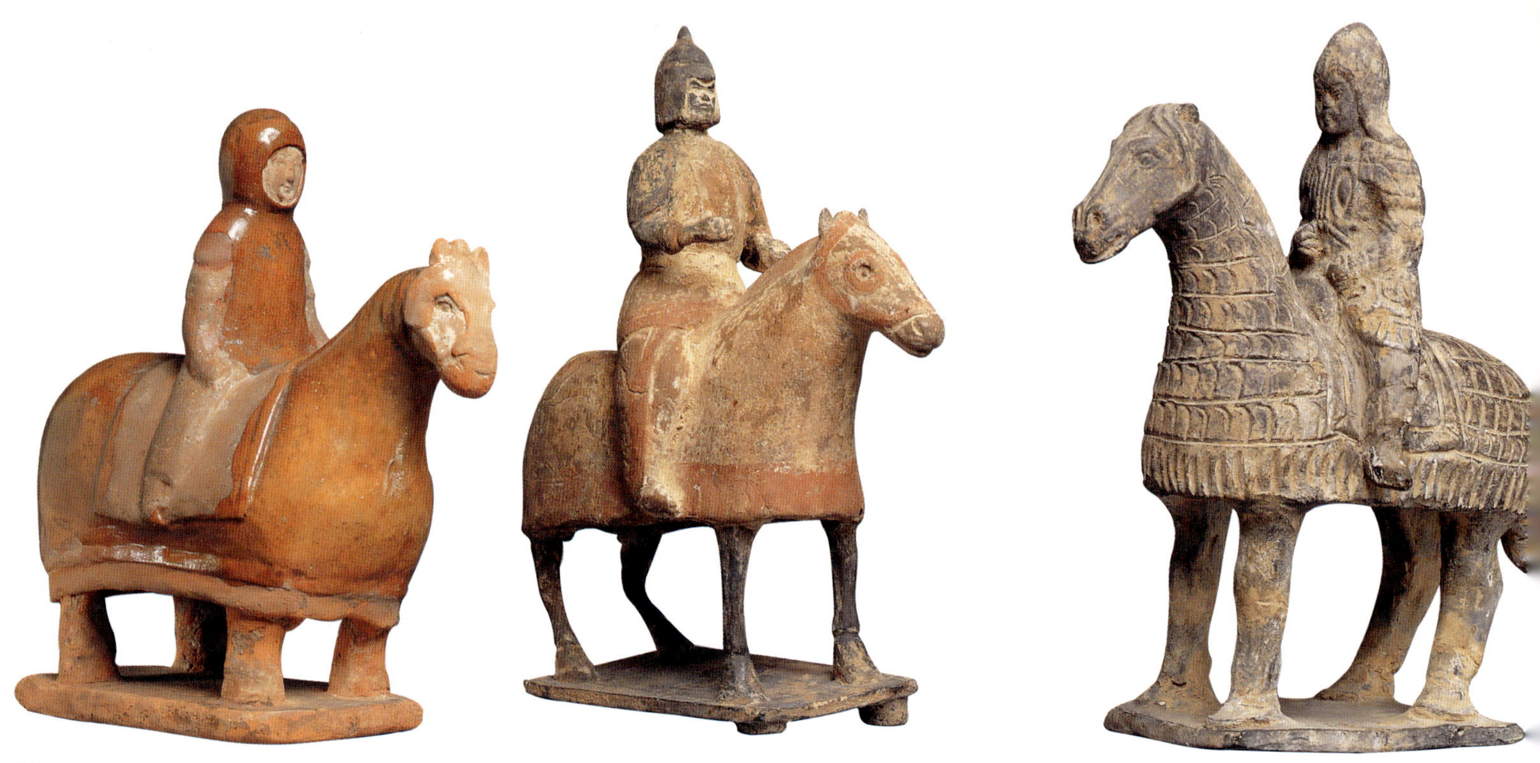

29.
Three armored equestrians
(Objects #103-105)

During this time, as warfare among China's different kingdoms increased, horse-breeding had become vital to serving military needs and armored horses became prevalent in *mingqi* as well. The practice of fitting horses with armor similar to that used by soliders but with the addition of a head mask, was introduced into China from Persia by way of Central Asia. Usually the shorter Mongolian ponies were fitted with armor. [6] Armor worn by soldiers became more complex. Innovations such as knee guards, longer belted armor tunics which covered the buttocks, helmets with ear protectors, multiple shoulder guards, and the use of shiny copper for the ensemble, resulted in the name *ming guang kai*, meaning "shining armor". These innovations along with the later addition of a knee-length skirt and suspended leg covers continued to be used. [7] (Figures 27-30)

30.
Pair of armored equestrians
(Object #106)

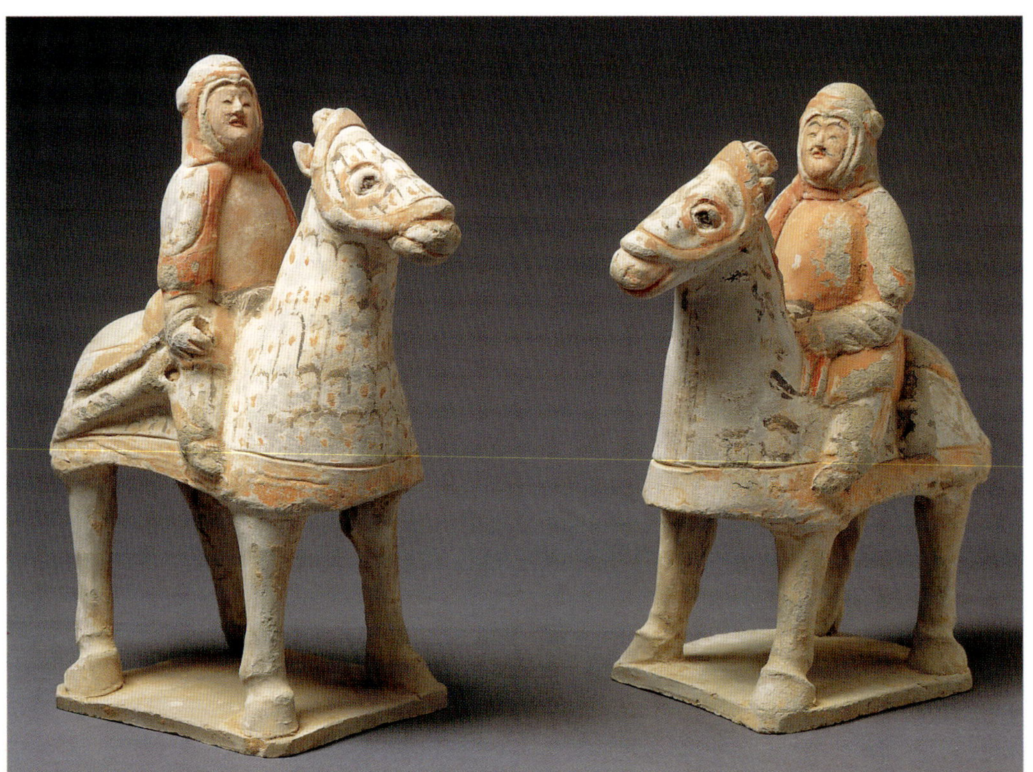

31.
Two equestrians
(Object #109)

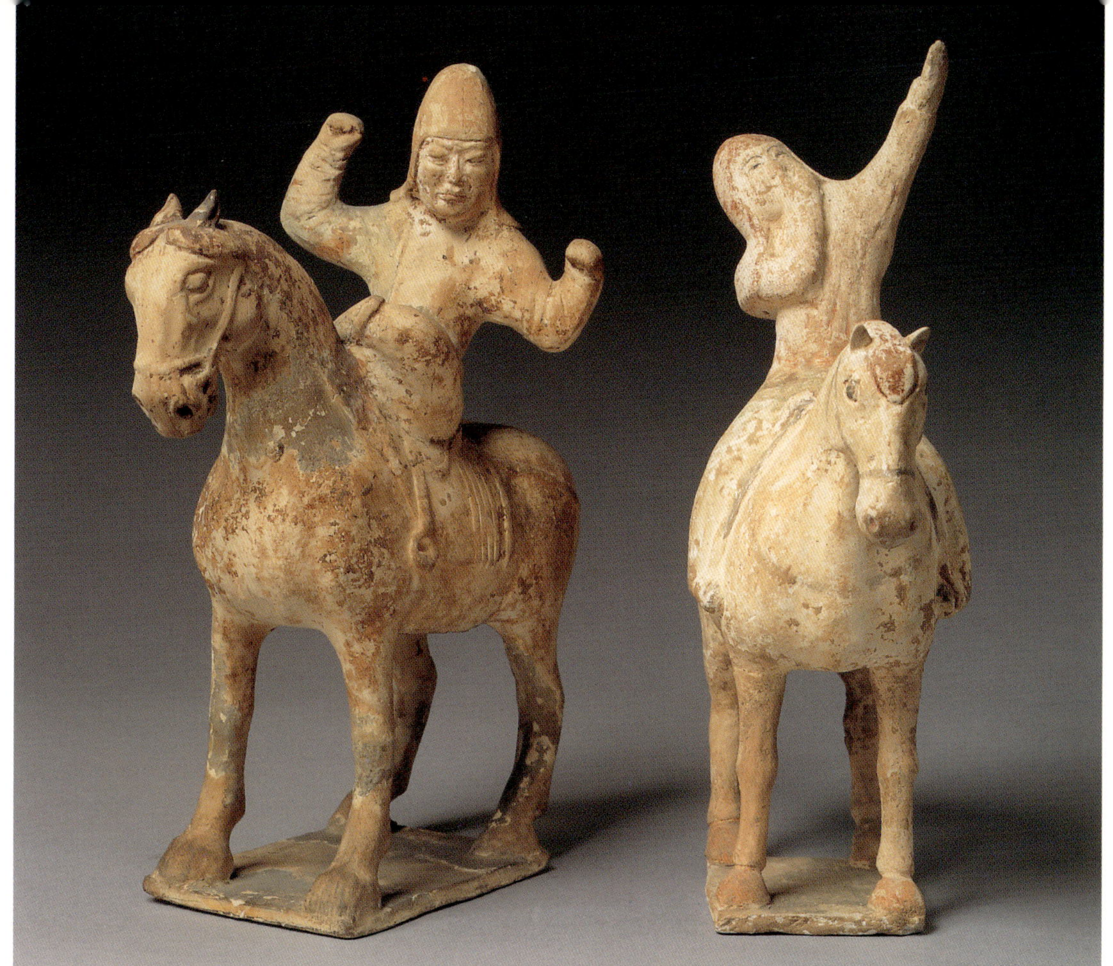

32.
Two equestriennes
(Object #108)

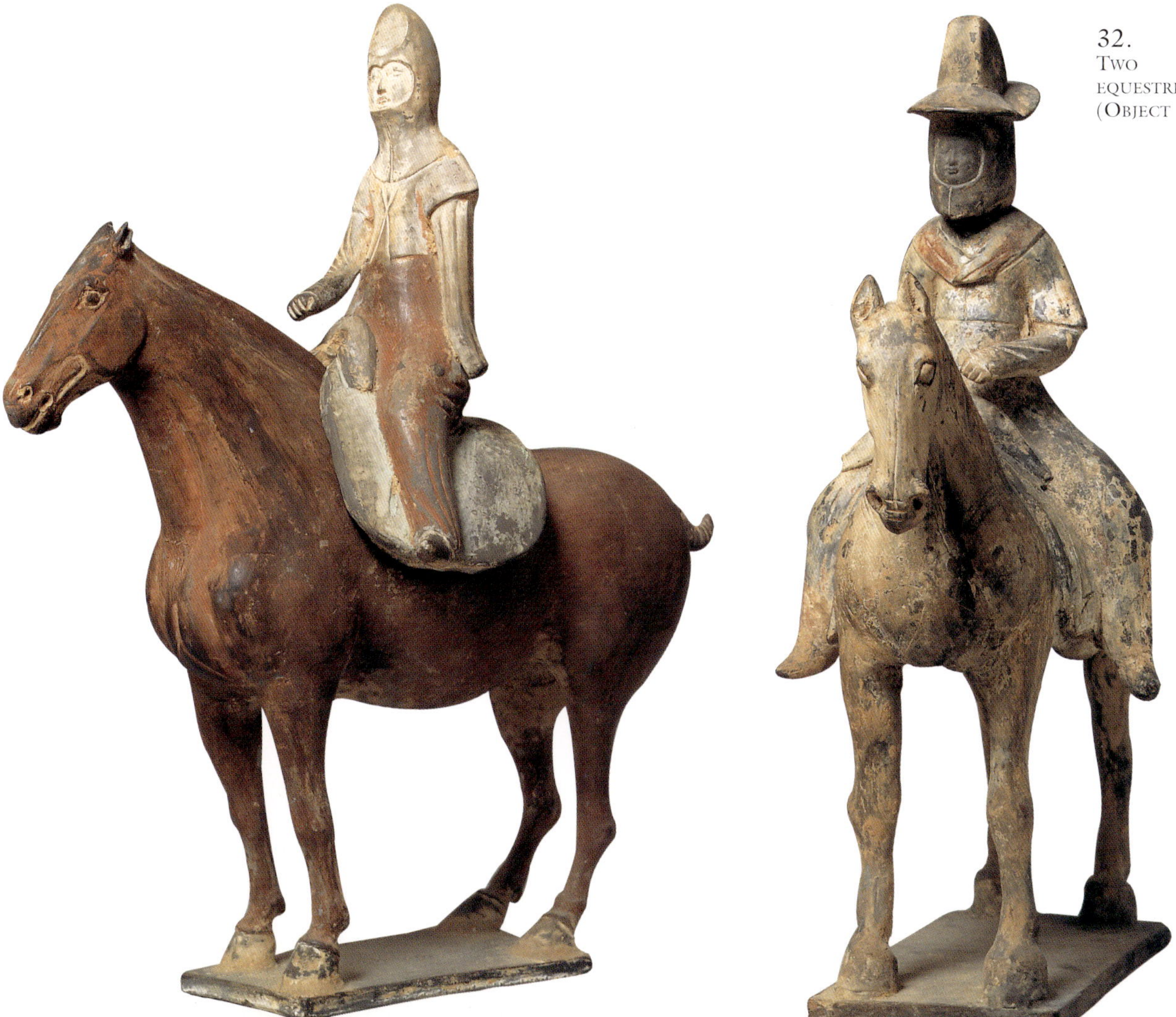

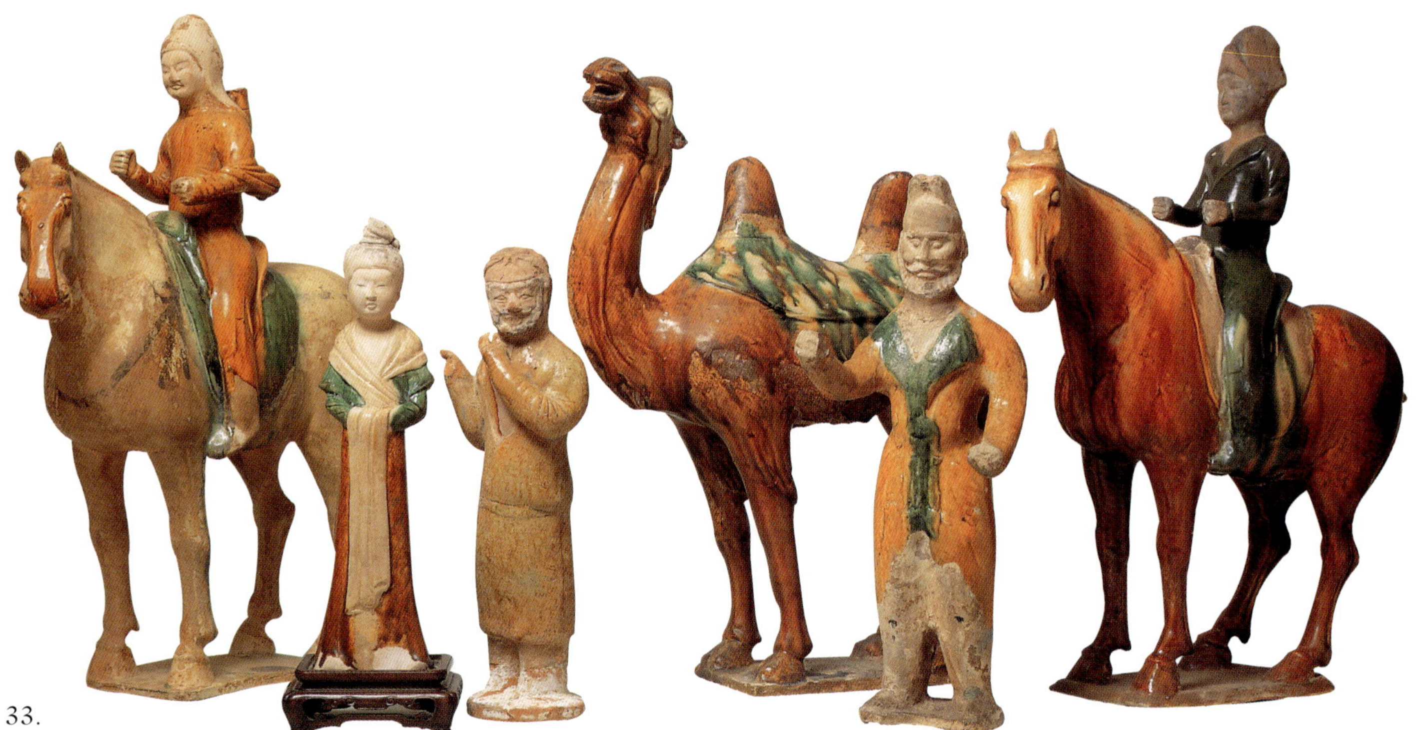

33.
Equestrian archer
(Object #131)
Court lady
(Object #132)
Foreign man playing a flute
(Object #133)
Bactrian camel
(Object #134)
Groom
(Object #135)
Equestrienne
(Object #136)

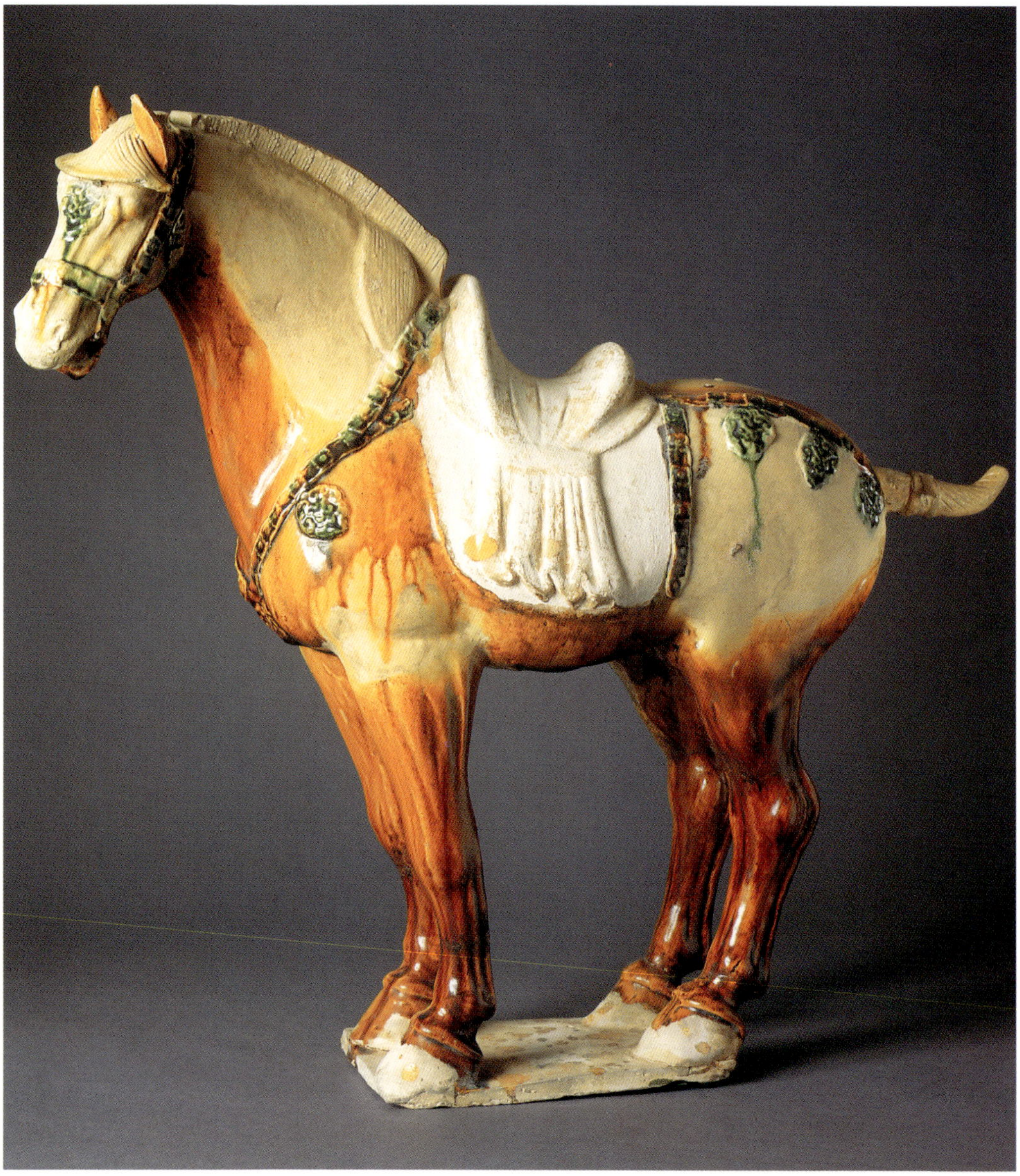

34.
Horse with saddle
(Object #137)

During the Sui and Tang periods, the peaceful rule that prevailed was instrumental in shifting the Emperor's interest in horses from the military to equestrian sports. The notion of horsemanship as an aristocratic privilege became linked with a fascination for travel and exotic lands. This combination brought about many portrayals of both Chinese and foreigners astride horses while hunting, playing musical instruments and enjoying the latest rage imported from Iran via Central Asia, the game of polo. [8] Since Tang women especially took to horseback riding, they adopted a novel costume of culottes, short capes, sun helmets and veiled hoods for comfort and protection against the elements. Historical documents evidence the relative amount of freedom women enjoyed during that time.

Tang aristocrats took great care in the ornamentation of their horses and *mingqi* feature braided manes and tails, beautiful medallions and other lavish accoutrements. Honor guards attended the horses of Tang emperors and princes of the Tang, outfitting them with pennants, light weapons and by tying their manes and tails into bunches to achieve a dramatic effect. (Figures 31-34) Perhaps the most legendary horses of the time were kept by Tang Emperor Minghuang (r. 712-756). His four hundred trained "dancing horses" reputedly entertained guests at his birthday celebrations by prancing to music on cue and drinking cups of wine during the performance. [9]

While the horse was undoubtedly the most celebrated and aristocratic animal in ancient Chinese society, the camel and ox also played important roles in transportation and travel. The two-humped Bactrian camel, known in China since Han times, was greatly prized

35.
Cart and Ox
(Object #114)
Pack horse
(Object #115)
Camel with pack
(Object #116)

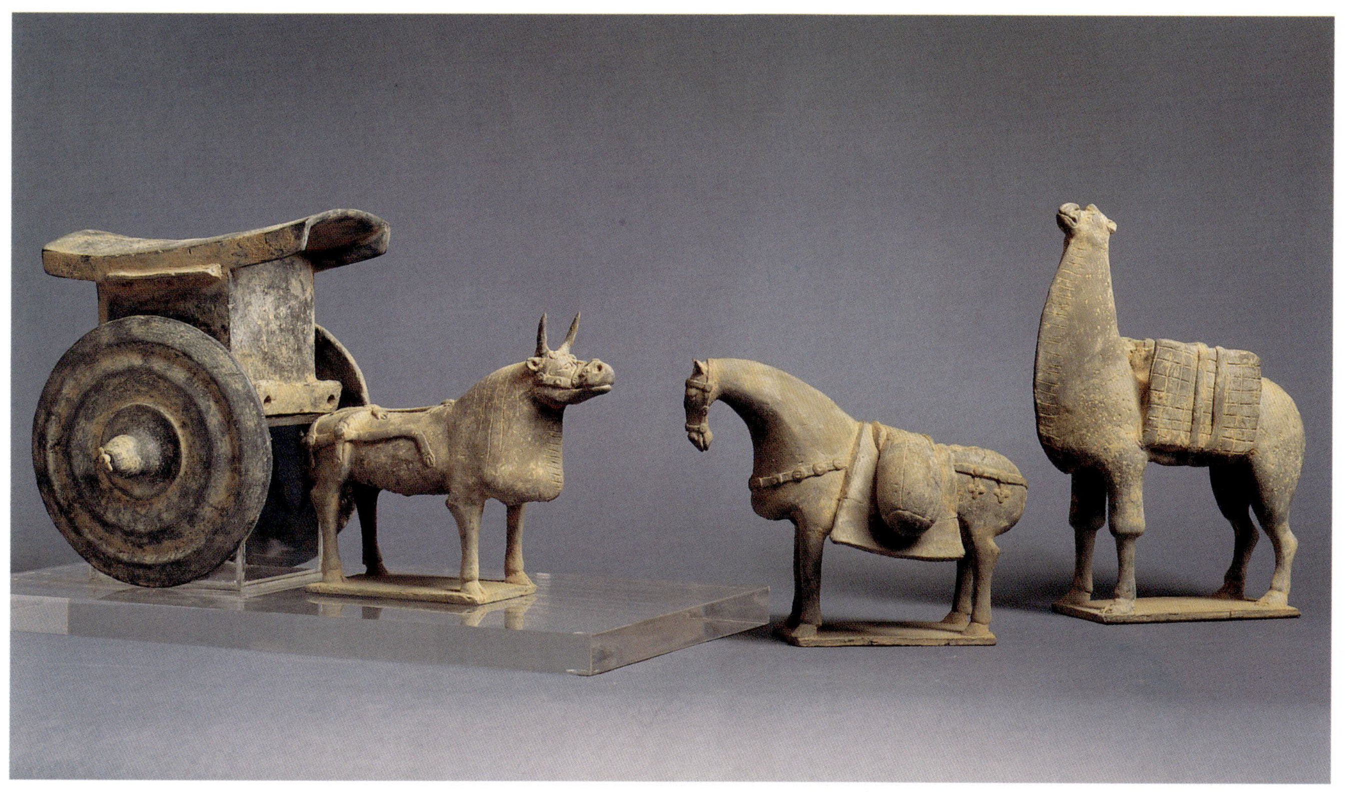

as a beast of burden along the treacherous deserts of the Silk Route. Camels, like horses, were acquired as tribute from the vast regions to the West of China's borders. While camel's hair was prized for its lightweight warmth, camel meat, particularly the hump, was consumed as a delicacy. [10] The camel's stubborn temperament has led to some humorous *mingqi* renderings of the beast. Servants and grooms who cared for and trained camels and horses were mostly foreigners, particularly horsemen from the Turkic tribes to China's northwest or herdsmen from Tibet.

The humble ox served several roles in ancient China as a beast of burden and transport as well as for agricultural cultivation. Like horses and camels, oxen seem to have been found in China from early times and in a variety of breeds, the "yellow ox" being the most commonly used as a beast of burden. [11] Its great strength and gentle disposition made it a valuable source of power in agriculture. In addition, the ox was also used to pull carts, and the frequent inclusion of oxcart *mingqi* in burials lends credence to the belief that oxcarts were an important part of funeral corteges during the Six Dynasties and Tang periods. [12] (Figures 35 & 36)

36.
CART AND BULL
(OBJECT #140)

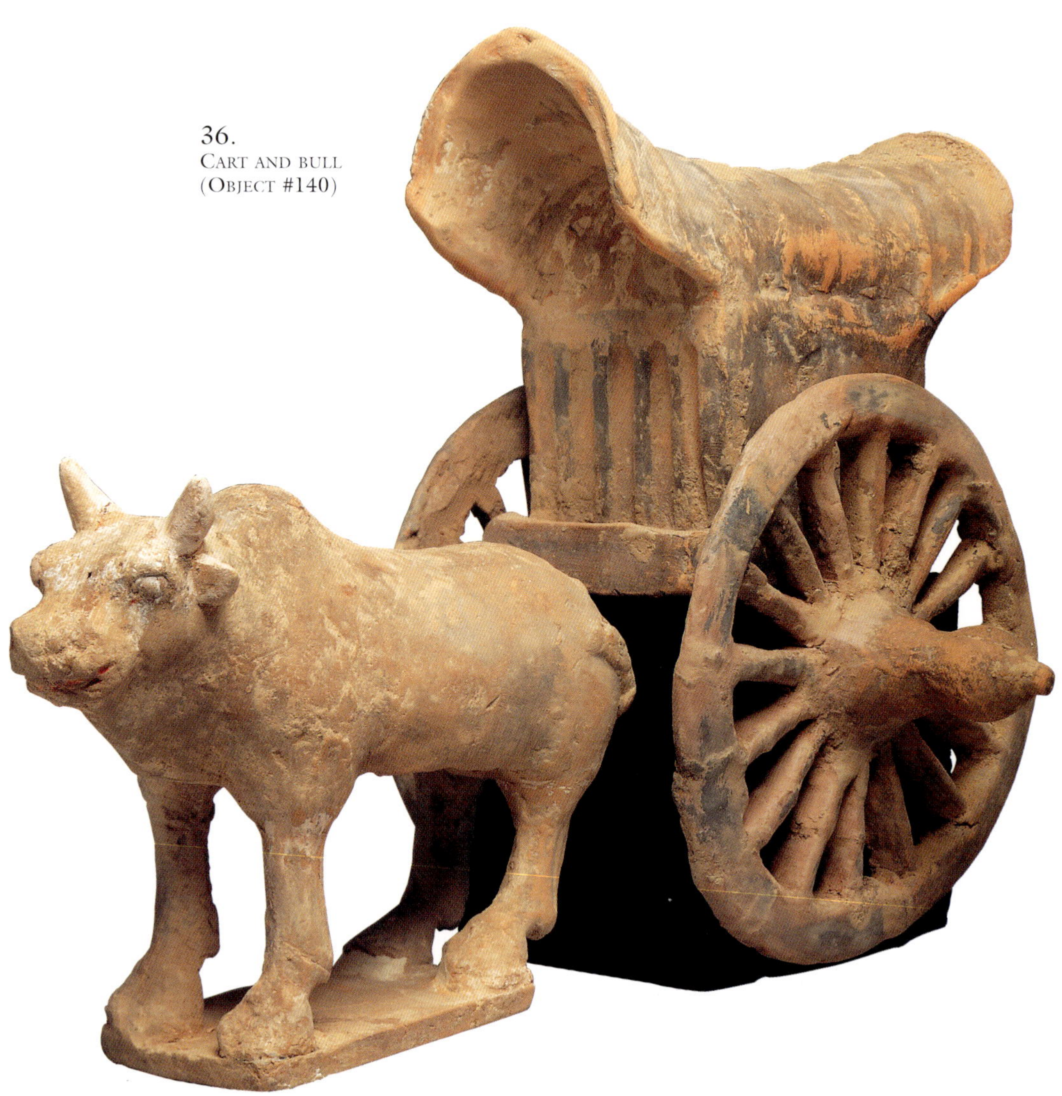

NOTES:

1. Wang Renbo, "General Comments on Chinese Funerary Sculpture," The Quest for Eternity, pp. 39-44. For sketches of the original color schemes of the different military costumes found in the Qin army, see Zhou Xun and Gao Chunming, 5000 Years of Chinese Costumes, pp. 47-51. See also the two-part article by Yang Hong, "Zhongguo Gudaide Jiazhou," Kaogu Xuebao, 1976, #1, pp. 19-46 and #2, pp. 59-95.

2. Michele Pirazzoli-t'Serstevens, The Han Dynasty, pp. 29-30.

3. Lucy Lim et al, Stories From China's Past, pp. 116-117.

4. Edward H. Schafer, The Golden Peaches of Samarkand: A Study of T'ang Exotics, pp. 58-70. See also Robert Temple, The Genius of China, pp. 89-90.

5. Lucy Lim et al, Stories From China's Past, pp. 146-147.

6. Albert E. Dien, "A Study of Early Chinese Armor," Artibus Asiae, 1981/82, Vol. 43, pp. 33-38.

7. Zhou Xun and Gao Chunming, 5000 Years of Chinese Costumes, pp. 70-71, 100-102.

8. Schafer, 66-67.

9. Ibid., pp. 67-69.

10. Ibid, pp. 70-72.

11. Ibid., pp. 73-75.

12. Kuwayama, "The Sculptural Development of Ceramic Funerary Figures in China," pp. 77-84.

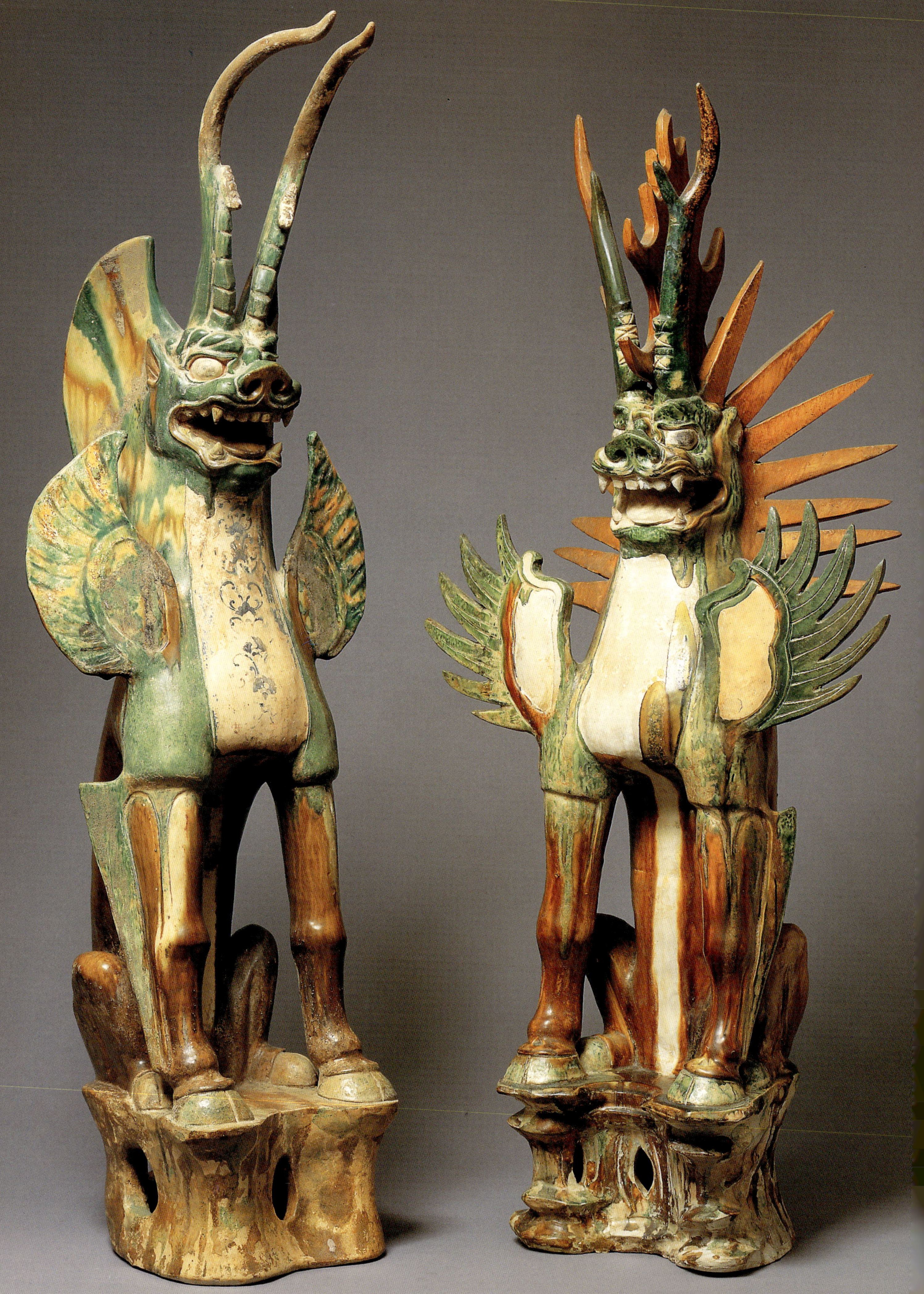

Mythical and Supernatural Beings

The majority of *mingqi* can be categorized as realistic since they are modelled on recognizable forms from everyday life. Nevertheless, there are several types of *mingqi* which are clearly more fantastic than realistic and exhibit intriguing combinations of human and animal features and the addition of multiple appendages mark these *mingqi* as fantastic. In some instances, the meaning or role of the figures is not clearly known. Some might have been created as an auspicious omen while others seem to have been designated as protectors to fend off evil spirits from the tomb and its occupants.

37.
FUXI AND NUWA
(OBJECT #146)

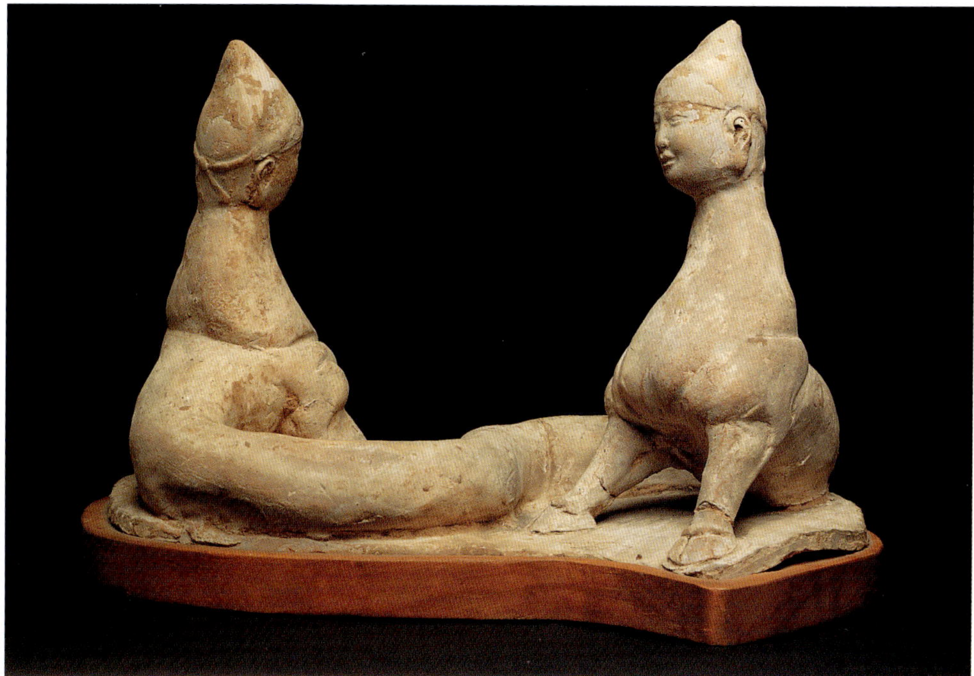

An image which appears in numerous examples of tomb murals and sculpture is that of the intertwined mythological deities of creation - Fuxi, a male and Nuwa, a female. Nuwa is credited with the creation of living beings, while Fuxi is regarded as the creator of the Daoist Eight Trigrams that reveal the natural order of Heaven and Earth. [1] Following the rise of the *yin-yang* theory, by which all elements in nature represent either the positive forces of radiance, heaven and masculinity or the negative forces of darkness, earth and femininity, these two figures were coupled together in pictorial images from the Han Dynasty which typically show the pair with human heads and symmetrically entwined serpentine bodies. The cosmic balance of *yin* and *yang* energy is manifest and controlled by Fuxi and Nuwa. In the Schloss example, their long serpentine tails mark them as spirits, while their pointed caps are of a type worn by educated bureaucrats in ancient China. (Figure 37) Thus, the specific significance of the Fuxi/Nuwa image is that of a moral nature. They symbolize the just rule of the Emperor over the realm through the fair recruitment of qualified scholars as government bureaucrats. Since benevolent rule of the Emperor would bring also bring about cosmic harmony through the balance of *yin* and *yang*, it can be concluded that images of Fuxi and Nuwa served as auspicious omens within the Chinese social order as well as in the cosmos. [2]

FACING PAGE: TWO TOMB GUARDIANS (OBJECT #149)

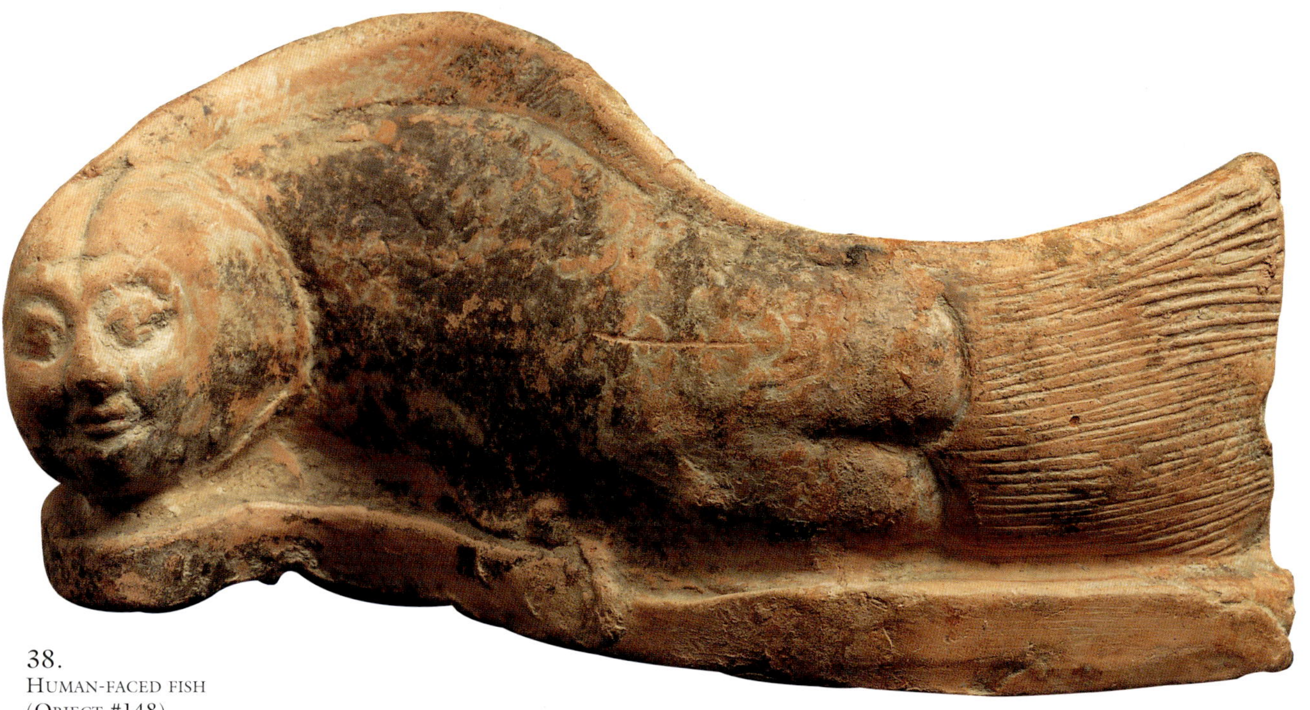

38.
Human-faced fish
(Object #148)

A second type of auspicious image is the human-headed fish. [3] Articulated in a curving S-shape evocative of its swimming motion, the fish is probably a carp. (Figure 38) In traditional Chinese symbolism, fish are associated with wealth or abundance because of the similar pronunciation of the words for wealth and fish (both are pronounced *yu*). Fish are also a symbol of marital harmony and regeneration, since they are said to swim in pairs. The carp, with its scaly armor, is regarded as a symbol of perseverance, since it swims against the current. [4] This fish, with its human face, is clearly a hybrid creature, and Han period tombs have revealed a variety of hybrid beasts and birds in which double or composite images signify the union of separate entities. The hybrid fish is said to appear when the ruler protects retired scholars. Like the omen of Fuxi and Nuwa, the hybrid fish implies that social harmony flourishes when the Emperor seeks and obtains the cooperation of worthy men. [5]

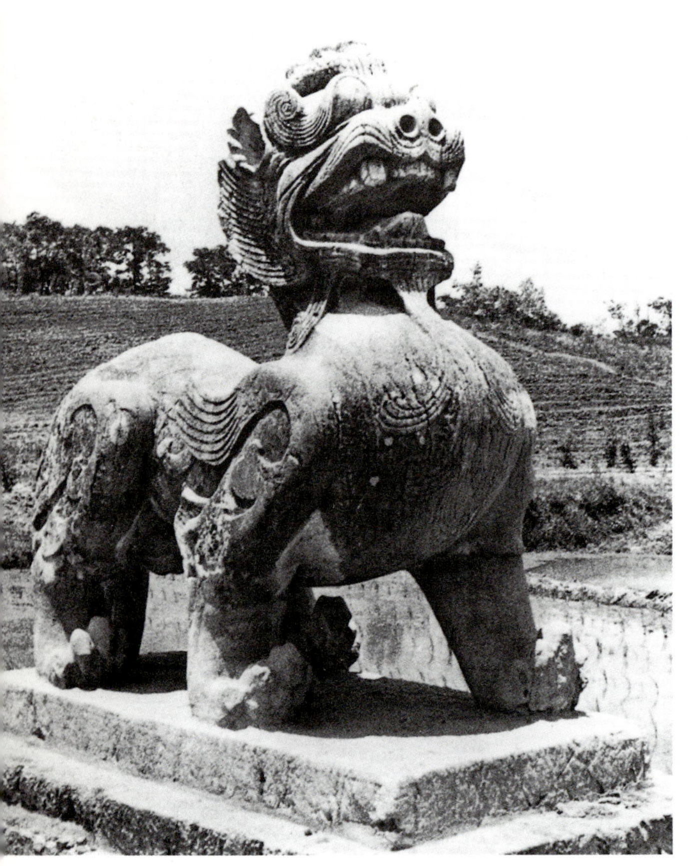

39.
Tomb guardian beast carved in stone, tomb of Emperor Chen Wendi, sixth century. In situ outside the city of Nanjing, Jiangsu province. From Liuchao Yishu, (1981).

Other beasts, some clearly fantastic and others quite naturalistic, were apparently created as ferocious guardians that fended off evil from the tomb. Beginning in the Han period, a type of winged feline creature is found in some tombs. A roaring mouth and staring eyes are typical features, indicating its fearsome nature. Large standing versions of such beasts, carved in stone, are found above the ground at many tomb sites of emperors of the Six Dynasties period (Figure 39) Combining powerful features of a lion, tiger and bird, their role was regarded as one of protector. Since its introduction into China when it was presented as a tribute gift from the Western kingdoms during the late Han period, the lion was traditionally designated as a guardian of the tomb. During the Six Dynasties period the promulgation of Buddhist art, where the lion is often shown

40.
Human-faced tomb guardian
(Object #144)

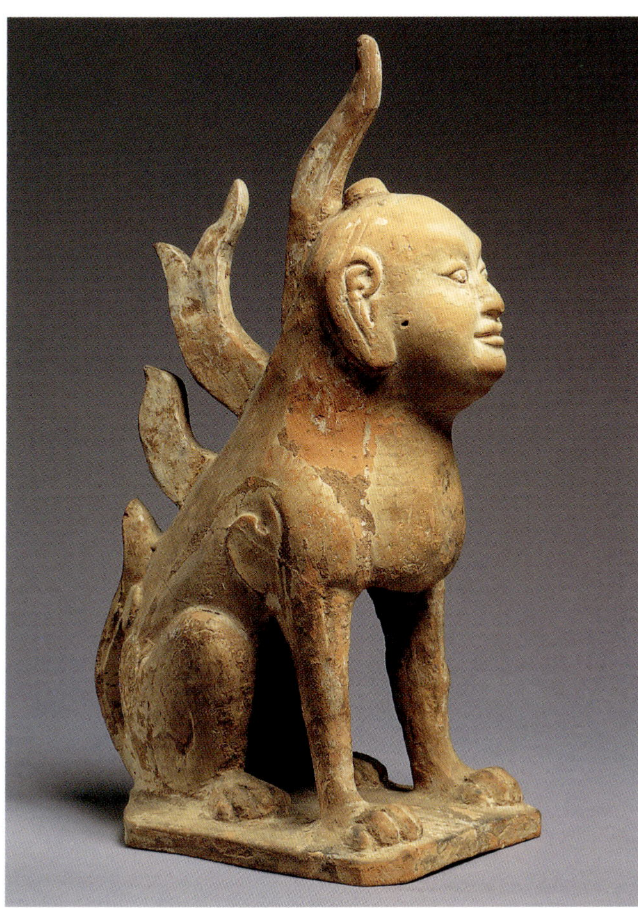

42.
Tomb guardian
(Object #151)

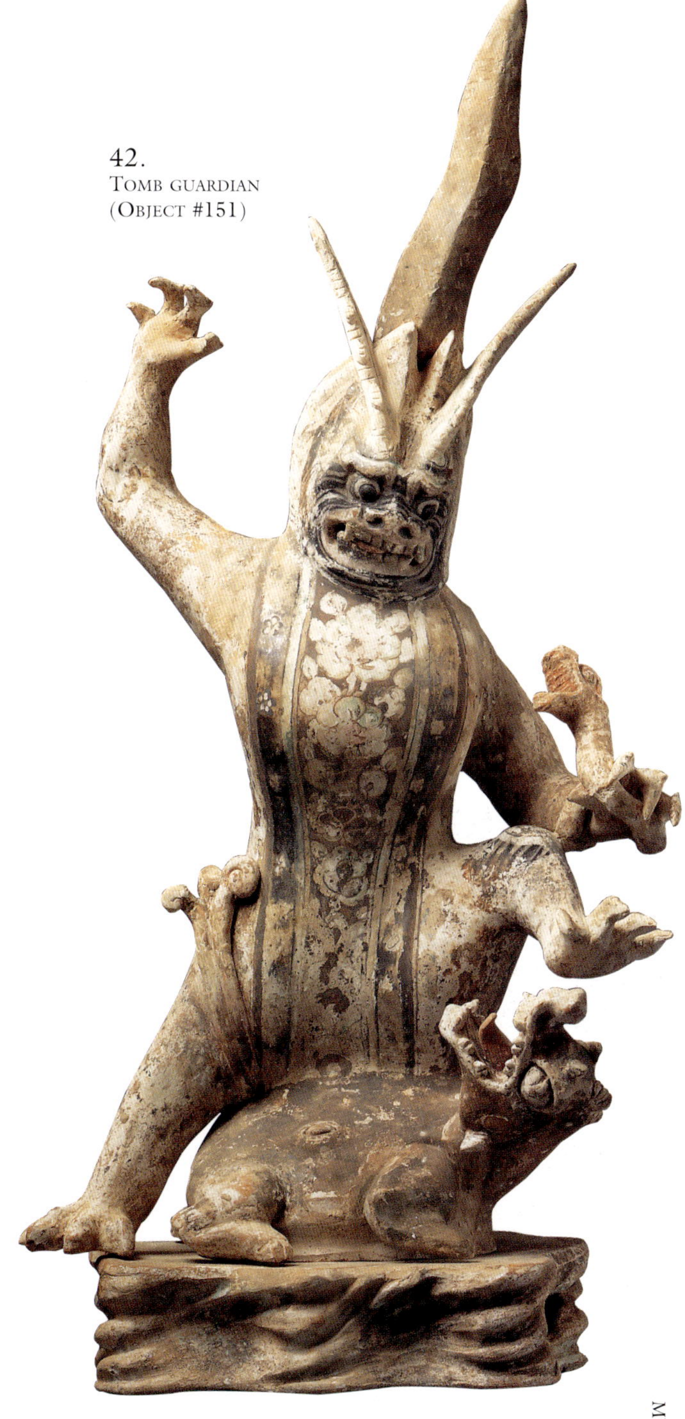

guarding the Buddha's throne, inspired first the emperor and then the nobility to adopt the regal creature as a tomb guardian. [6]

Such composite beasts have been called by a variety of terms in English and Chinese, including chimera, *guaishou* (strange animal), or *tianlu* (heavenly deer). Currently, the correct Chinese term for such beasts is *zhenmushou*, literally "tomb guardian creature." [7] During the Six Dynasties period, ceramic *mingqi* versions of this composite beast begin to appear inside the tombs, often in pairs with one having a human face and the other having an animal face, usually that of a lion. In some instances they have cloven hooves, like those of a deer, rather than lion's paws. Although pointed horns on their heads and spiky flanges along their backs indicate their supernatural power, these creatures are often endowed with benevolent, even smiling faces. However, during the Sui and Tang periods, *zhenmushou* become increasingly dramatic and fearsome. Multiple horns, fangs, tentacles and wings along with clenched fists and grimacing facial expressions heighten their power to ward off evil spirits. Rendered in large scale and embellished with vivid colors, these figures effectively convey their supernatural power to conquer evil. Here, the artists' creativity has conjured up images

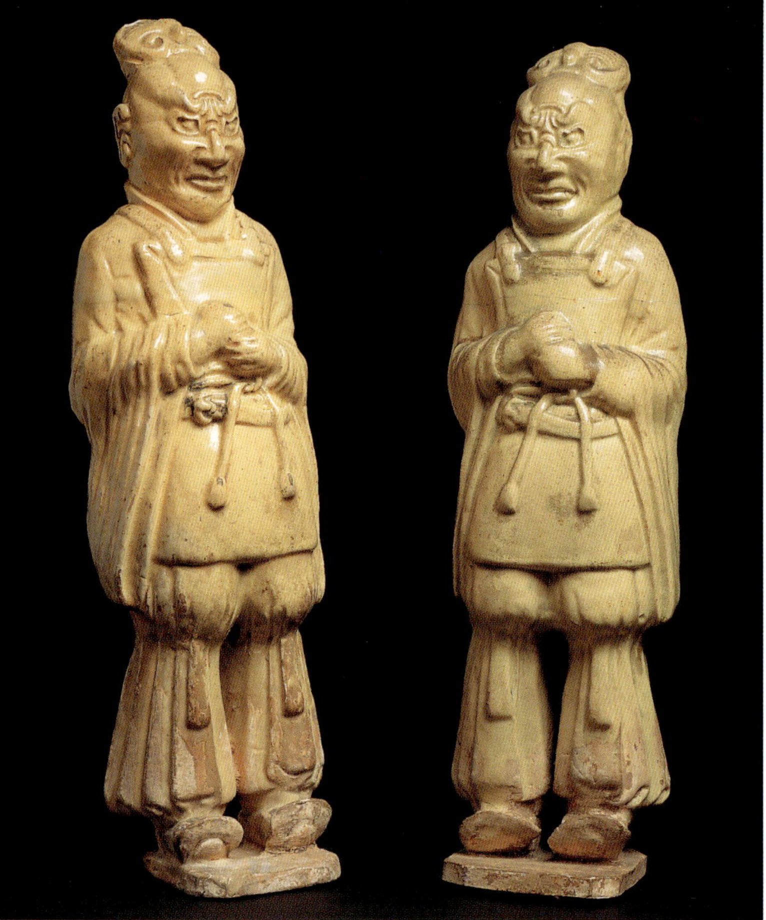

that certainly did not exist in the everyday world. (Figures 40 & 41)

The second type of guardian figure which appears in Chinese tombs is that of the tomb guardian soldier, called in Chinese *zhenmuyong*. Beginning in the Han Dynasty but flourishing during the Six Dynasties period, these ferocious human soldier figures were found in pairs, usually dressed in the *mingguangkai* ("bright shining") armor and carrying a large shield. Clearly modelled on contemporary soldiers, pairs of this type of figure were found along with the *zhenmushou* creatures, thus comprising a well-established group of four guardian figures in the tomb. However, during the Sui and Tang periods, when the internal unrest and warfare had subsided, a new kind of guardian figure replaced the *zhenmuyong* soldiers. These new figures do not carry a shield and wear long robes under their elaborately ornamented armor. Impractical for

41.
Pair of tomb guardian soldiers
(Object #121)

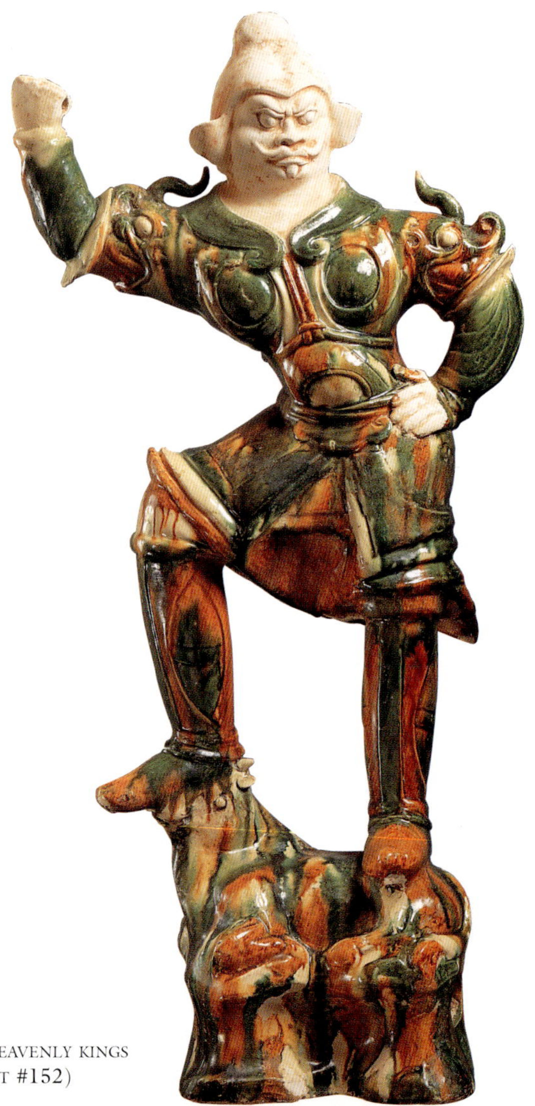

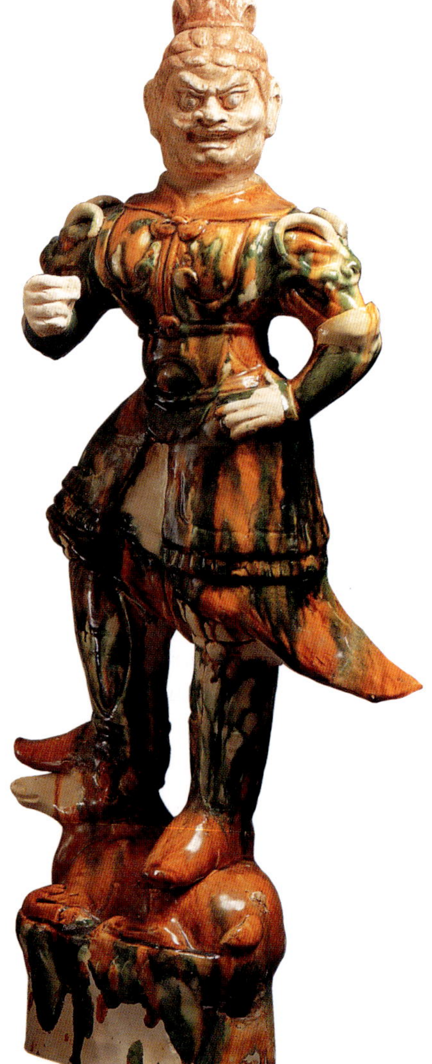

43.
Two heavenly kings
(Object #152)

combat, this type of military costume probably was modelled after the palace guards of the Tang imperial household, guarding the tomb in the afterlife as they would have guarded the palace in real life. [8] (Figure 42)

Yet this type of guardian was soon replaced by another still more vivid guardian image, that of the *tianwangyong*, or Heavenly King. Modelled after various Buddhist cult images, such as the Four Lokapalas or Guardians of the Four Cardinal Directions, the grimacing Heavenly Kings are warriors posed aggressively upon a demonlike dwarf or a recumbent ox, symbolizing evil averted. Such images are often found outside of the entrance to Buddhist temples, where they fend off evil spirits from the throne of the Buddha. [9] Thus, this final version of the guardian warrior, the Heavenly King, constitutes a fusion of earlier examples of tomb guardian warriors with Buddhist iconographical influence by protecting the burial site from evil spirits emanating from the four directions. The Heavenly Kings are usually found together with pairs of the *zhenmushou* tomb guardian creatures, representing a culmination of the variety and multiplicity of fantastic images designed to carry the deceased safely to his final destination in the next world. (Figures 43 & 44)

Notes:

1. Michael Lowe, Chinese Ideas of Life and Death, pp. 64-72.
2. Martin J. Powers, Art and Political Expression in Early China, pp. 253-254.
3. I wish to thank Virginia Bower for her insight on the many variations and recently excavated examples of the hybrid fish motif which, unfortunately, this essay does not permit further discussion.
4. C.A.S. Williams, Outlines of Chinese Symbolism and Art Motives, pp. 183-186.
5. Martin J. Powers, pp. 257-260.
6. Mary H. Fong, "Tomb Guardian Figures: Their Evolution and Iconography," Ancient Mortuary Traditions of China, pp. 84-93.
7. Ibid., pp. 84-97.
8. Ibid., pp. 93-98.
9. Robert L. Thorp, Son of Heaven, p. 200.

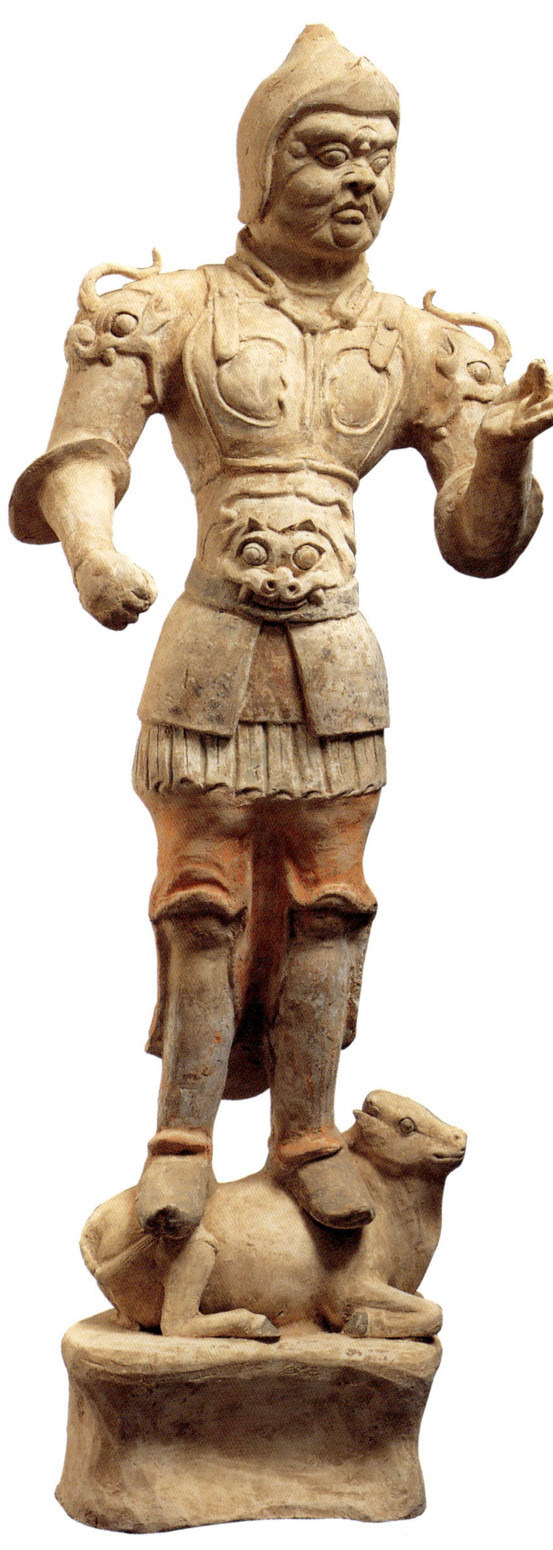

44.
Heavenly king
(Object #153)

Exhibition Checklist with Archaeological Comparisons

Architecture, Agriculture & Domestic Life

1. Tower with moat
Earthenware with light green glaze
37" (95 cm.) high
Eastern Han Dynasty (25-220 AD)

Comparative archaeological examples - a group of similar towers were found in Eastern Han tombs at Zhangwan, Lingbao County, Henan province; see Wenwu, 1975, #11, pp. 75-93.

2. Tower
Earthenware with light green glaze
25 1/2" (65 cm.) high
Eastern Han Dynasty (25-220 AD)

Comparative archaeological examples - a similar tower was found in Han tombs of the Yang family at Diaochao, Tongguan, Shaanxi province; see Wenwu, 1961, #1, p. 61, fig. 23.

3. Tower with moat
Earthenware with light green glaze
30" (76 cm.) high
Eastern Han Dynasty (25-220 AD)

4. Tower with moat
Earthenware with dark green glaze
31" (79 cm.) high
Eastern Han Dynasty (25-220 AD)

Comparative archaeological examples - a nearly identical tower was found in an Eastern Han tomb at Sanshengwan, Lingbao County, Henan province; see Kaogu Tongxun, 1957, #4, pl. 3: 3&4.

5. Tower with moat
Earthenware with dark green glaze
24" (61 cm.) high
Eastern Han Dynasty (25-220 AD)

6. Tower with moat
Earthenware with dark green glaze
24" (61 cm.) high
Eastern Han Dynasty (25-220 AD)

7. Farmhouse
Unglazed pottery
9" (23 cm.) high
Eastern Han Dynasty (25-220 AD)

Comparative archaeological examples - similar farmhouses were found in Eastern Han tombs in Wuzhou, Guangxi province; see Wenwu, 1972, #2, p. 71, fig. 3; and at Zhuanshishan, Nanjing, Jiangsu province; see Kaogu Tongxun, 1956, #4, figs. 9:1 and 10:3.

8. Barn with dog
Unglazed pottery
8" (22 cm.) high
Han Dynasty (206 BC-220 AD)

9. Farmhouse with two figures
Unglazed pottery
7 3/4" (20 cm.) high
Han Dynasty (206 BC-220 AD)

10. Animal pen with figure and tower
Earthenware with green glaze
12" (31 cm.) high
Han Dynasty (206 BC-220 AD)

Comparative archaeological examples - a group of similar pens with small towers was found in a group of undated Han tombs in Xinye County, Henan province; see Kaogu Xuebao, 1990, #4, figs. 4:4-6.

11. Goat pen
Earthenware with green glaze
3 1/2" (8.5 cm.) high
Eastern Han Dynasty (25-220 AD)

Comparative archaeological examples - an identical pen was found in the Eastern Han tombs at Zhangwan, Lingbao County, Henan province; see Wenwu, 1975, #10, p. 91, fig. 48.

12. Pen with goats being fed
Earthenware with green glaze
5 3/4" (14.5 cm.) high
Han Dynasty (206 BC-220 AD)

13. Pig
Earthenware with green glaze
3" (7.5 cm.) high
Eastern Han Dynasty (25-220 AD)

Comparative archaeological examples - identical figures were found in the Eastern Han tombs at Zhangwan, Lingbao County, Henan province; see Wenwu, 1975, #10, p. 91, fig. 50.

14. Pig pen with privy
Earthenware with green glaze
9 1/2" (24 cm.) high
Eastern Han Dynasty (25-220 AD)

Comparative archaeological examples - an identical pen was found in the Eastern Han tombs at Zhangwan, Lingbao County, Henan province; see Wenwu, 1975, #10, p. 91, fig. 46.

15. Scene of grain hulling with human figure and dog
Earthenware with light green glaze
4 1/2" (11 cm.) high
Western Han Dynasty (206 BC-8 AD)

Comparative archaeological examples - a similar grain huller was found, in combination with a grain winnower, in the Western Han tombs at Sijiangou, Jiyuan County, Henan province; see Wenwu, 1973, #2, 46-53; and in the Eastern Han sacrificial tomb at Dongguan, Luoyang, Henan province; see Wenwu, 1973, #2, pp. 55-60, fig. 2.

16. Cylindrical granary
Earthenware with greenish-yellow glaze
10" (25.5 cm.) high
Eastern Han Dynasty (25-220 AD)

Comparative archaeological examples - similar examples were found in the Han tombs at Xintongqiao, Zhengzhou, Henan province; see Wenwu 1972, #10, p. 41, fig. 1.

17. Wellhead
Earthenware with green glaze
11" (28 cm.) high
Han Dynasty (206 BC-220 AD)

18. Wellhead
Earthenware with yellow glaze
14" (36 cm.) high
Eastern Han Dynasty (25-220 AD)

Comparative archaeological examples - a similar wellhead, but with a suspended bucket, was found in the group of Eastern Han tombs at Zhangwan, Lingbao County, Henan province; see Wenwu, 1975, #10, p. 88, fig. 23; a square wellhead of similar design was found in the sacrificial Eastern Han tomb at Dongguan, Luoyang; see Wenwu, 1973, #2, p. 62, fig. 13.

19. Wellhead with Animals of the Four Directions
Gray unglazed pottery
4 1/4" (10.5 cm.) high
Late Western (206 BC-8 AD) or early Eastern Han (25-220 AD) Dynasty

20. Wellhead with dragon and tiger relief designs
Gray unglazed pottery
4" (10 cm.) high
Late Western (206 BC-8 AD) or early Eastern Han (25-220 AD) Dynasty

Comparative archaeological examples - a wellhead similar to #20 and #21, but with abstract relief designs, was found in a Han tomb at Shaogou, Luoyang, Henan province; see Wang Zhongshu, Han Civilization, p. 56, pl. 73. Similar relief designs of the directional animals have been found on impressed clay bricks used to build late Western Han tombs; see Wenwu, 1972, #10, p. 48, figs. 3 and 19.

21. Watchdog
Earthenware with dark green glaze
8 1/4" (21 cm.) high
Eastern Han period (25-220 AD)

Comparative archaeological examples - a very similar watchdog, but with his mouth open as though barking, was found in the group of Eastern Han tombs at Zhangwan, Lingbao County, Henan province; see Wenwu, 1975, #10, p. 91, fig. 51; and in a Han tomb at Laodaosi, Mian county, Shaanxi; see Kaogu, 1985, #5, pp. 429-449, fig. 4:8.

22. Ox with trappings
Gray unglazed pottery
6" (15 cm.) high
Six Dynasties, Northern Qi period (550-577 AD)

Comparative archaeological examples - similar figures were found in a Northern Qi tomb, dated 550, at Dongchengcun, Cixian, Hebei province; see Wenwu, 1974, #4, pl. 5, fig. 1; and in the Northern Qi tomb at Nanjiao, Taiyuan, Shanxi province; see Wenwu, 1990, #2, p.9, pl. 14, fig. 3.

23. Chewing dog
Gray unglazed pottery
2 1/4" (6 cm.) high
Six Dynasties, Northern Wei period (386-535 AD)

Comparative archaeological examples - an identical figure was found in a Northern Wei tomb, dated 524, at Quyang, Hebei province; see Kaogu, 1972, #5, p. 34, fig. 1.

24. Reclining dog
Gray unglazed pottery
3 1/2" (9 cm.) high
Six Dynasties, Northern Qi period (550-577 AD)

Comparative archaeological examples - a very similar figure found in the Northern Qi tomb of Gao Run, dated 576 AD, at Cixian, Hebei province; see Kaogu, 1979, #3, p. 240, pl. 6, fig. 6.

25. Ram
Gray unglazed pottery
5 3/4" (14.5 cm.) high
Six Dynasties, Northern Wei period (386-535 AD)

Comparative archaeological examples - a very similar figure was found in a Northern Wei tomb, dated 524, at Quyang, Hebei province; see Kaogu, 1972, #5, p. 34, fig. 1.

26. Horse
Gray pottery with white slip
9 1/4" (23.5 cm.) high
Late Eastern Han Dynasty (25-220 AD) or early Six Dynasties (386-581 AD)

Comparative archaeological examples - a horse of similar form, but with bridle and saddle, was found in a third century tomb at Zhengzhou, Henan province; see Kaogu Tongxun, 1957, #3, pl. 44.

27. Pig
Gray unglazed pottery
4" (10 cm.) high
Six Dynasties, Northern Wei period (386-535 AD)

Comparative archaeological examples - a very similar figure was found in the Northern Wei tomb dated 524 AD at Quyang, Hebei province; see Kaogu, 1972, #5, p. 34, fig. 1.

28. Ox
Gray pottery with white slip
4 3/4" (12 cm.) high
Late Eastern Han Dynasty (25-220 AD) or early Six Dynasties (386-581 AD)

Comparative archaeological examples - an identical figure was found in a pair of tombs dated to the third century at Xingyuancun, Yanshi County, Henan province; see Kaogu, 1985, #8, fig. 16, pl. 17:7.

29. Rooster
Gray pottery with white slip and pigment traces
6 1/4" (16.5 cm.) high
Late Eastern Han Dynasty (25-220 AD) or early Six Dynasties (386-581 AD)

Comparative archaeological examples - similar figures were found in the Eastern Han tombs at Zhangwan, Lingbao County, Henan province; see Wenwu, 1975, #10, p. 91, fig. 49; in third century tombs at Zhengzhou, Henan province; see Kaogu Tongxun, 1957, #1, pl. 14:6; and in third century tombs at Xingyuancun, Yanshi County, Henan province; see Kaogu, 1985, #8, pl. 18:1.

30. Hen with chick
Gray unglazed pottery
7" (18 cm.) high
Late Eastern Han Dynasty (25-220 AD) or early Six Dynasties (386-581 AD)

31. Rooster
Earthenware with green glaze
8" (20.5 cm.) high
Eastern Han Dynasty (25-220 AD)

Comparative archaeological examples - similar figures were found in the Eastern Han tombs at Zhangwan, Lingbao County, Henan province; see Wenwu, 1975, #10, p. 91, fig. 49.

32. Boar
White pottery with straw-colored glaze
3 1/2" (6.5 cm.) high
Six Dynasties, Northern Qi period (550-577 AD)

Comparative archaeological examples - an identical figure was found in the Northern Qi tomb of Gao Run, dated 576, at Cixian, Hebei province; see Wenwu, 1979, #3, p. 240, pl. 6, fig. 10.

33. Seated dog
White pottery with dark green glaze
4 3/4" (12 cm.) high
Tang Dynasty (618-906 AD)

34. Sleeping dog
White pottery with yellow glaze
3 3/4" (9.5 cm.) high
Tang Dynasty (618-906 AD)

35. Rooster
White pottery with three-colored glazes
2 1/2" (6 cm.) high
Tang Dynasty (618-906 AD)

Comparative archaeological examples - very similar figures were found in the Tang tomb of Dugu Sizhen, dated 697, near Xian, Shaanxi province; see Tang Chang'an Chengjiao Suitangmu, pl. LVI, fig. 1.

36. Duck
White pottery with three-colored glazes
2 1/2" (6.5 cm.) high
Tang Dynasty (618-906 AD)

Comparative archaeological examples - similar figures in the Tang tomb of Dugu Sizhen, dated 697, near Xian, Shaanxi province; see Tang Chang'an Chengjiao Suitangmu, pl. LVI, fig. 2.

37. Eight women doing chores
Gray pottery with white slip
4 1/2" (11.5 cm.) height of tallest figure
Six Dynasties, Northern Wei period (386-535 AD)

Comparative archaeological examples - a very similar set of five ladies was found in the Northern Wei tomb of Cui Hong, dated 525 AD, at Linzi, Shandong province; see Kaogu Xuebao, 1984, #2, pl. 1, fig. 1.

38. Stove with vessel
Gray unglazed pottery
9" (23 cm.) high
Han Dynasty (206 BC-220 AD)

Comparative archaeological examples - very similar stoves were found in the group of undated Han tombs at Xingye, Henan province; see Kaogu Xuebao, 1990, #4, pl. 5, fig. 1-5.

39. Stove with relief designs
Earthenware with green glaze
3 1/2" (8 cm.) high
Eastern Han Dynasty (25-220 AD)

Comparative archaeological examples - a similar stove was found in the late Eastern Han tombs at Zhangwan, Lingbao County, Henan province; see Wenwu, 1975, #10, p. 88, fig. 26; and in the Han tomb at Xinmang, Yanshi, Luoyang, Henan province; see Wenwu, 1992, #12, p. 7, fig. 17.

40. Stove with chimney
Earthenware with brown glaze
8 1/2" (21.5 cm.) high
Eastern Han Dynasty (25-220 AD)

41. Cricket roaster
Earthenware with green glaze
5 1/2" (14 cm.) high
Han Dynasty (206 BC-220 AD)

42. Dish with bird
Gray unglazed pottery
6 1/2" (16.5 cm.) high
Han Dynasty (206 BC-220 AD)

43. Incense burner
Earthenware with green glaze
3 1/2" (9 cm.) high
Eastern Han Dynasty (25-220 AD)

Comparative archaeological examples - a very similar burner was found in the group of Eastern Han tombs at Zhangwan, Lingbao County, Henan province; see Wenwu, 1975, #10, p. 89, fig. 30.

44. Dragon-handled dish
Earthenware with green glaze
5 1/2" (14 cm.) high
Han Dynasty (206 BC-220 AD)

45. Dragon-handled ladle
Earthenware with green glaze
5 1/2" (14 cm.) long
Han Dynasty (206 BC-220 AD)

46. Hill-jar censer
Earthenware with dark green glaze
10 1/4" (25 cm.) high
Eastern Han Dynasty (25-220 AD)

Comparative archaeological examples - a nearly identical example was found in the Eastern Han tomb at Liujiaqu, Shan County, Henan province; see Kaogu Xuebao, 1965, #1, p. 126, fig. 18:3.

47. Ceramic imitation of a covered bronze tripod vessel
Earthenware with dark green glaze
8 1/4" (21 cm.) high
Han Dynasty (206 BC-220 AD)

Comparative archaeological examples - similar vessels were found in the undated Han tombs at Xinye, Henan province; see Kaogu Xuebao, 1990, #4, pl. 3, figs. 1-3.

48. Money box, shown with 17 bronze coins
Gray unglazed pottery
6 1/2" (16.5 cm.) high
Eastern Han Dynasty (25-220 AD)

Comparative archaeological examples - a similar money box, but with feet, was found in the group of Eastern Han tombs at Zhangwan, Lingbao County, Henan province; see Wenwu, 1975, #10, p. 87, fig. 18.

Social And Cultural Life

49. Two nude figures (left female, right male)
Unglazed pottery with white slip and pigment traces
Left 21 1/4" (54 cm.), right 24" (61 cm.) high
Western Han Dynasty (206 BC-8 AD)

Comparative archaeological examples - similar pottery figures were found in a side pit to the mausoleum of Jingdi, Western Han emperor who reigned 156-141 BC, at Xian, Shaanxi province; see Wenwu, 1992, #4, pp. 1-13, figs. 1-5. Small bronze belthooks were found next to them, suggesting that the figures were originally dressed in fabric clothes.

50. Dancer
Gray unglazed pottery
11" (28 cm.) high
Western Han Dynasty (206 BC-8 AD)

51. Pair of female attendants
Gray pottery with pigment traces
10 1/2" (26 cm.) high
Western Han Dynasty (206 BC-8 AD) or Warring States period (476-221 BC)

Comparative archaeological examples - similar figures were found in a Western Han tomb found at Linyi, Shandong province; see Wenwu, 1974, #2, p. 22, figs. 13 & 14, p. 25, figs. 14 & 15; and in a Warring States tomb at Zidanku, Changsha, Hunan province; see Wenwu, 1974, #2, pp. 36-40, figs. 13-14.

52. Gentleman
Gray pottery with pigment traces
13 3/4" (35 cm.) high
Western Han Dynasty (206 BC-8 AD)

Comparative archaeological examples - similar figures were found in a group of Western Han tombs at Hongqing Village, Xian, Shaanxi province; see Kaogu, 1959, #12, pp. 662-67, figs. 1-3.

53. Pair of ladies
Gray pottery with pigment traces
12" (30.5 cm.) high
Western Han Dynasty (206 BC-8 AD)

Comparative archaeological examples - similar figures were found in the group of Western Han tombs at Hongqing Village, Xian, Shaanxi province; see Kaogu, 1959, #12, pp. 662-67, figs. 1-3.

54. Dancer
Gray pottery with white slip
5 1/4" (13.5 cm.) high
Western Han Dynasty (206 BC-8 AD)

Comparative archaeological examples - a similar figure was found in a Western Han tomb at Sijiangou, Jiyuan County, Henan province; see Wenwu, 1973, #2, pp. 46-53; and in the Eastern Han sacrificial tomb at Dongguan, Luoyang, Henan province; see Wenwu, 1973, #2, pp. 55-60, fig. 2.

55. Seated zither player
Gray pottery with white slip
5" (13 cm.) high
Eastern Han Dynasty (25-220 AD)

Comparative archaeological examples - very similar figures were found in an Eastern Han tomb at Gulugou, Xinan County, Henan province; see Kaogu, 1966, #3, pp. 133, 134, 137; and in the Eastern Han tomb at Qilihe, Jianxi, Luoyang, Henan province; see Kaogu, 1975, #2, pp. 116-123, fig. 5.

56. Seated mother and child
Gray pottery with white slip
5" (13 cm.) high
Eastern Han Dynasty (25-220 AD)

57. Storyteller
Gray pottery with white slip
4 1/2" (11.5 cm.) high
Eastern Han Dynasty (25-220 AD)

Comparative archaeological examples - a similar figure was excavated from an Eastern Han tomb at Luoyang, Henan province; see The Chinese Exhibition, figs. 212-217.

58. Pair of musicians
Gray pottery with white slip and pigment traces
3 1/2" (9 cm.) high
Eastern Han Dynasty (25-220 AD)

59. Dancer
Gray pottery with white slip and pigment traces
3 1/2" (9 cm.) high
Eastern Han Dynasty (25-220 AD)

Comparative archaeological examples - similar figures were found in an Eastern Han tomb at Qilihe, Jianxi, near Luoyang, Henan province; see Kaogu, 1975, #2, pp. 116-134, fig. 2.

60. *Liubo* players
Gray pottery with pigment traces
4 3/4" (12 cm.) height of taller figure
Eastern Han Dynasty (25-220 AD)

Comparative archaeological examples - a similar pair of figures, mounted on a platform, was found in a late Eastern Han group of tombs at Zhangwan, Lingbao County, Henan province; see Wenwu, 1975, #11, p, 89, fig. 35.

61. Dancer
Unglazed gray pottery
8" (20.5 cm.) high
Eastern Han Dynasty (25-220 AD)

Comparative archaeological examples - a nearly identical figure was found in an Eastern Han tomb at Luoyang, Henan province; see The Chinese Exhibition, figs. 212-217.

62. Brick with relief depicting juggler
Gray unglazed pottery
7 1/2" (19 cm.) high
Eastern Han Dynasty (25-220 AD)

Comparative archaeological examples - similar pottery bricks were found in an Eastern Han tomb at Peng County, Sichuan province; see Stories From China's Past, p. 144, pl. 49.

63. Two court ladies
Gray pottery with white slip and pigment traces
6" (15.5 cm.) height of taller figure
Six Dynasties, Northern Wei period (386-535 AD)

Comparative archaeological examples - a similar figure was found in the Northern Wei tomb of Yuan Shao, dated 528, at Kuoyang, Henan province; see Kaogu, 1973, #4, p. 220, fig. 4.

64. Twins
Gray pottery with white slip and pigment traces
6 1/4" (16 cm.) high
Six Dynasties, Northern Wei period (386-535 AD)

65. Dancer
Gray pottery with pigments
6 1/2" (16.5 cm.) high
Six Dynasties, Northern Wei period (386-535 AD)

66. Two musicians
Gray pottery with pigment traces
7 3/4" (19.5 cm.) height of taller figure
Six Dynasties, Northern Wei period (386-535 AD)

67. Pair of officials
Gray pottery with white slip and pigment traces
14 1/2" (36.5 cm.) high
Six Dynasties, Northern Wei period (386-535 AD)

Comparative archaeological examples - similar figures were found in the Northern Wei tomb of Yuan Shao, dated 524, at Luoyang, Henan province; see Kaogu, 1973, #4, p. 219, figs. 1-4.

68. Official
Gray pottery with white slip and pigment traces
14 1/2" (36.5 cm.) high
Six Dynasties, Western Wei period (535-557 AD)

Comparative archaeological examples - very similar figures were found in a Western Wei tomb at Cuijiaying, Hanzhong, Shaanxi province; see Kaogu yu Wenwu, 1981, #2, pp. 21-24, pls. 11-13.

69. Soldier
Gray pottery with white slip and pigment traces
12" (30.5 cm.) high
Six Dynasties, Northern Wei period (386-535 AD)

Comparative archaeological examples - a similar figure was found in a Northern Wei tomb dated 524, at Quyang, Hebei province; see Kaogu, 1972, #5, pl. 10:11.

70. Group of seven court ladies, three musicians and a dancer
White pottery with clear glaze and pigment traces
9" (22 cm.) height of tallest figure
Sui (581-618 AD) or early Tang Dynasty (618-906 AD)

Comparative archaeological examples - identical figures were found in the Tang tomb at Dasikong Village, Anyang, Henan province, datable to approximately 642 AD; see Kaogu, 1955, #5, pp. 5-54, pl. 1:4.

71. Musician and dancer
White pottery with clear glaze and pigment traces
10" (25 cm.) high
Sui Dynasty (581-618 AD)

Comparative archaeological examples - very similar figures were found in the Sui tomb of Princess Li Jingxun, dated 608, near Xi'an, Shaanxi province; see Kaogu, 1959, #9, pp. 471-479, also Tang Chang'an Chengjiao Suitangmu, pp. 3-27, pls. 21:1 & 2.

72. Girl
White pottery with straw-colored and green glazes
7 3/4" (18 cm.) high
Sui (581-618 AD) or early Tang Dynasty (618-906 AD)

73. Court lady
White pottery with green glaze and pigments
9 1/4" (23.5 cm.) high
Sui (581-618 AD) or early Tang Dynasty (618-906 AD)

74. Pair of court ladies, one holding a musical instrument
Red pottery with olive green glaze and pigments
9 3/4" (24.5 cm.) high
Early Tang Dynasty (618-906 AD)

Comparative archaeological examples - similar figures were found in the Tang tomb of Zheng Rentai, datable to 664, at Liquan County, near Xi'an, Shaanxi province; see Wenwu, 1972, #7, p. 33-41, pls. 1:1 and 3:3.

75. Servant
White pottery with clear glaze and pigment traces
11" (23 cm.) high
Early Tang Dynasty (618-906 AD)

Comparative archaeological examples - a similar figure was found in the Tang tomb of Zhang Shigui, dated 657, at Liquan County, near Xi'an, Shaanxi province; see Kaogu, 1978, #3, pp. 168-178, pls. 1:6-8.

76. Servant
White pottery with straw-colored glaze and pigment traces
8" (20.5 cm.) high
Sui (581-618 AD) or early Tang Dynasty (618-906 AD)

Comparative archaeological examples - an identical figure was found in a Tang tomb, datable to 642, at Dasikong Village, near Anyang, Henan province; see Kaogu, 1955,#5, pp. 50-54, pl. 1:3.

77. Man wearing overcoat
White pottery with straw-colored glaze and pigment traces
7 3/4" (19.5 cm.) high
Sui (581-618 AD) or early Tang Dynasty (618-906 AD)

Comparative archaeological examples - identical figures were found in a Tang tomb, datable to 642, at Dasikong Village, near Anyang, Henan province; see Kaogu, 1955, #5, pp. 50-54, pls. 2:1 & 2.

78. Servant
White pottery with pigments
8 1/4" (21 cm.) high
Early Tang Dynasty (618-906 AD)

Comparative archaeological examples - a similar figure was found in the Tang tomb of Zhang Shigui, dated 657, at Liquan County, near Xi'an, Shaanxi province; see Kaogu, 1978, #3, pp. 168-178, pls. 1:6-8.

79. Official
White pottery with clear glaze
8 1/2" (21.5 cm.) high
Early Tang Dynasty (618-906 AD)

Comparative archaeological examples - a similar figure was found in the Tang tomb of Zhang Shigui, dated 657, at Liquan County, near Xi'an, Shaanxi province; see Kaogu, 1978, #3, pp. 168-178, pl. 1:1.

80. Pair of foreign attendants
White pottery with clear glaze and pigment traces
9 1/2" (24 cm.) high
Sui (581-618 AD) or early Tang Dynasty (618-906 AD)

81. Foreign attendant
White pottery with clear glaze
10 1/4" (25.5 cm.) high
Sui (581-618 AD) or early Tang Dynasty (618-906 AD)

82. Pair of foreign attendants
White pottery with clear glaze and pigment traces
10 1/2" (26 cm.) high
Sui (581-618 AD) or early Tang Dynasty (618-906 AD)

83. Trio of seated musicians
White pottery with pigment traces
6 1/4" (16 cm.) high
Sui (581-618 AD) or early Tang Dynasty (618-906 AD)

Comparative archaeological examples - similar figures were found in a Tang tomb, datable to 642, at Dasikong Village, near Anyang, Henan province; see Kaogu, 1955, #4, pp. 50-54, pls. 1:4 & 5; and in the tomb of Zhang Sheng, dated 595, at Anyang, Henan province; see Kaogu, 1959, #10, pp. 541-545, pls. 2:1-6. A group of six seated female musicians in similar poses but with different hairstyle and costume was found in a Tang tomb, dated 701, at Xishantou, Mengjin, Luoyang, Henan province; see Wenwu, 1992, #3, pp. 1-8, fig. 1:1-6.

84. Foreign dancer
White pottery with straw-colored glaze and pigment traces
12 1/2" (31 cm.) high
Early Tang Dynasty (618-906 AD)

85. Four court ladies
White pottery with pigment traces
12 1/2" (31.5 cm.) height of tallest figure
Early Tang Dynasty (618-906 AD)

Comparative archaeological examples - very similar figures were found in the Tang tomb of Zhang Shigui, date 657, at Liquan County, near Xi'an, Shaanxi province; see Kaogu, 1978, #3, pp. 168-178, pls. 4:3 & 6; in the tomb of Zheng Rentai, dated 664, at Liquan County, near Xi'an, Shaanxi province; see Wenwu, 1972, #7, pp. 38-41, pl. 1:1 and 3:3; and in the Tang tomb of Liu Kai and his wife, dated 664, at Yanshi, Henan province; see Wenwu, 1992, #12, p. 24, fig. 6, p. 28, fig. 18 & 19. A lady with a high peaked hairstyle like the far right figure was found in the Tang tomb, dated 701, at Xishantou, Mengjin, Luoyang, Henan province; see Wenwu, 1992, #3, pp. 1-8, fig. 5:3.

86. Five court ladies
White pottery with three-colored glazes
11" (28 cm.) height of tallest figure
Tang Dynasty (618-906 AD)

Comparative archaeological examples - similar figures were found in the Tang tomb of General Anpu, dated 709, at Longmen, near Luoyang, Henan province; see Zhongyuan Wenwu, 1982, #3, pp. 21-26pls. 4:7-9; and in a Tang tomb, dated 701, at Xishantou, Mengjin, Luoyang, Henan province; see Wenwu, 1992, #3, pp. 1-8, fig. 5:4&5.

87. Four court ladies
Red pottery with white slip and pigment traces
19" (48 cm.) height of tallest figure
Tang Dynasty (618-906 AD)

Comparative archaeological examples - very similar figures were found in the Tang tomb of Wu Shouzhong, dated 748, at Gaolou Village, near Xi'an, Shaanxi province; see Wenwu Cankao Ziliao, 1955, #7, pp. 103-109; and in a group of Tang tombs in the western suburbs of Xi'an; see Kaogu yu Wenwu, 1991, #4, pl. 18:1-4, 8-12, and Wenwu, 1992, #9, pls. 2 & 3.

88. Seven foreign men
White pottery with olive green glaze and pigment traces
14" (36 cm.) height of tallest figure
Tang Dynasty (618-906 AD)

Comparative archaeological examples - similar figures were found in the Tang tomb of General Anpu, dated 709, at Longmen, near Luoyang, Henan province; see Zhongyuan Wenwu, 1982, #3, pl. 3:7 & 9; in the Tang tomb of Prince Zhanghuai, dated 706, at Qian County, near Xi'an, Shaanxi province; see Wenwu, 1972, #7, pp. 13-25; and in the Tang tomb of Dugu Sizhen, dated 697, near Xi'an, Shaanxi province; see Tang Chang'an Chengjiao Suitangmu, pl. LXV.

89. Two officials
White pottery with three-colored glazes
28 1/2" (72 cm.) height of taller figure
Tang Dynasty (618-906 AD)

Comparative archaeological examples - very similar figures were found in the Tang tomb of General Anpu, dated 709, at Longmen, near Luoyang, Henan province; see Zhongyaun Wenwu, 1982, #3, pl. 3:1; in the Tang tomb of Prince Zhanghuai, dated 706, near Xi'an, Shaanxi province; see Wenwu, 1972, #7, pl. 5; and in the Tang tomb of Dugu Sizhen, dated 697, near Xi'an, Shaanxi province; see Tang Chang'an Chengjiao Suitangmu, pls. XLII:1 & 2.

Military, Sport And Transportation

90. Horse
Earthenware with pigment traces
23" (58.5 cm.) high
Western Han Dynasty (206 BC-8 AD)

Comparative archaeological examples - identical horses, but with riders, were found in the tomb of the first Han emperor, Gaozu and the tomb of Han emperor Jingdi at Yangjiawan, Xianyang, Shaanxi province; see Wenwu, 1966, #3, pp. 1-5 and Wenwu, 1977, #10, p. 10ff.

91. Pair of soldiers
Earthenware with white slip and pigment traces
18" (46 cm.) high
Western Han Dynasty (206 BC-8 AD)

Comparative archaeological examples - similar figures, but holding shields, were found in the Western Han tomb at Yangjiawan, Xianyang, Shaanxi province; see Wenwu, 1966, #3, pp. 1-5, figs. 1-4; and in the Western Han tomb at Langjiagou, Xianyang, Shaanxi province; see Kaogu, 1981, #5, 422-425.

92. Soldier
Gray pottery with traces of white slip
17" (43.5 cm.) high
Six Dynasties, Western Jin period (265-316 AD)

Comparative archaeological examples - a very similar figure was found in the Western Jin tomb at Zhengzhou, Henan province; see Kaogu Tongxun, 1957, #1, pls. 14:3-6.

93. Pair of officials
Gray pottery with pigment traces
10 1/2" (26.5 cm.) high
Six Dynasties, Northern Wei period (386-535 AD)

Comparative archaeological examples - an identical figure was found in the Northern Wei tomb of Gao Ya, dated 537, at Jing County, Hebei province; see Wenwu, 1979, #3, p. 26, pl. 16.

94. Pair of soldiers with shields
Gray pottery with pigment traces
10 3/4" (27.5 cm.) high
Six Dynasties, Northern Wei period (386-535 AD)

Comparative archaeological examples - a very similar figure was found in the Northern Wei tomb of Gao Zhangming, dated 548, at Jing County, Hebei province; see Wenwu, 1979, #3, p. 28, pl. 27.

95. Two soldiers
Red pottery with white slip, pigment and gilt traces
19" (48.5 cm.) height of taller figure
Six Dynasties, Northern Qi period (550-577 AD)

Comparative archaeological examples - very similar figures were found in the Northern Qi tomb of Kudi Huailo, dated 562, at Shouyang County, Shanxi province; see Kaogu Xuebao, 1979, #3, pl. 4:1; and in the Northern Qi tomb near Taiyuan, Shanxi province; see Wenwu, 1990, #12, pl. 2:3 & 4.

96. Two footsoldiers
Gray pottery with white slip and pigment traces
8 1/4" (22 cm.) high
Six Dynasties, Northern Wei period (386-535 AD)

Comparative archaeological examples - identical figures were found in the Northern Wei tomb of Yuan Shao, dated 528, at Luoyang, Henan province; see Kaogu, 1973, #4, p. 219, fig. 3.

97. Kneeling soldier
Gray pottery with white slip and pigment traces
7" (18 cm.) high
Six Dynasties, Northern Wei period (386-535 AD)

98. Man wearing overcoat
Gray pottery with pigment traces
7 1/4" (18.5 cm.) high
Six Dynasties, Northern Wei period (386-535 AD)

Comparative archaeological examples - similar figures were found in the Northern Wei tomb of Yuan Shao, dated 528, at Luoyang, Henan province; see Kaogu, 1973, #4, p. 219, pl. 3, fig. 1.

99. Female attendant
Gray pottery with white slip and pigment traces
8 1/4" (20.5 cm.) high
Six Dynasties, Northern Wei period (386-535 AD)

Comparative archaeological examples - similar figures were found in the Northern Wei tomb of Yuan Shao, dated 528, at Luoyang, Henan province; see Kaogu, 1973, #4, p. 220, pl. 5, figs. 1-3.

100. Two officials
Gray pottery with white slip and pigment traces
8 1/4" (20.5 cm.) height of taller figure
Six Dynasties, Northern Wei period (386-535 AD)

Comparative archaeological examples - nearly identical figures were found in the Northern Wei tomb of Yuan Shao, dated 528, at Luoyang, Henan province; see Kaogu, 1973, #4, p. 219, pl. 4, figs. 1-4.

101. Mule with saddle
Gray pottery with white slip and pigment traces
5" (12.5 cm.) high
Six Dynasties, Northern Wei period (386-535 AD)

Comparative archaeological examples - a similar mule, but with saddlebags instead of a saddle, was found in a Northern Wei tomb, dated 524, at Quyang, Hebei province; see Kaogu, 1972, #5, pl. 3:1; and in the Northern Wei tomb of Yuan Shao, dated 528, at Luoyang, Henan province; see Kaogu, 1973, #4, p. 221, fig. 8.

102. Pack horse
Gray pottery with white slip and pigment traces
5 1/2" (14 cm.) high
Six Dynasties, Northern Wei period (386-535 AD)

Comparative archaeological examples - a very similar figure was found in the Northern Wei tomb of Yuan Shao, dated 528, at Luoyang, Henan province; see Kaogu, 1973, #4, p. 221, fig. 8; a pack horse of similar style was found in the Northern Wei tomb of Gao Ya, dated 537, at Jing County, Hebei province; see Wenwu, 1979, #3, p. 27, fig. 24.

103. Armored equestrian
Red pottery with yellow-brown glaze
9" (23 cm.) high
Six Dynasties, Northern Wei (386-535 AD) or Eastern Wei period (534-550 AD)

Comparative archaeological examples - a similar figure was found in the Northern Wei tomb of Sima Jinlong, dated ca. 470, at Datong, Shanxi province; see Wenwu, 1972, #3, pp. 20-33; and in the Eastern Wei tomb of Li Xizhong, dated 540; see Kaogu, 1977, #6, pl. VII: 4.

104. Armored equestrian
Gray pottery with white slip and pigment traces
10 1/4" (26 cm.) high
Six Dynasties, Northern Wei period (386-535 AD)

Comparative archaeological examples - a very similar figure was found in the Northern Wei tomb of Yuan Shao, dated 528, at Luoyang, Henan province; see Kaogu, 1973, #4, pl. 3:2.

105. Armored equestrian
Gray pottery
10 1/4" (26 cm.) high
Six Dynasties, Northern Qi period (550-577 AD)

Comparative archaeological examples - a very similar figure was found in the Northern Qi tomb of Gao Run, dated 576, at Cixian, Hebei province; see Kaogu, 1979, #3, pp. 235-244, pl. 4, fig. 5.

106. Pair of armored equestrians
Gray pottery with pigments
11" (28 cm.) height of taller figure
Six Dynasties, Northern Qi period (550-577 AD)

107. Three equestrian drummers and one armored equestrian
Gray pottery with white slip and pigment traces
9 1/2" (24 cm.) height of tallest figure
Six Dynasties, Northern Wei period (550-577 AD)

Comparative archaeological examples - very similar figures were found in the Northern Wei tomb of Yuan Shao, dated 528, at Luoyang, Henan province; see Kaogu, 1973, #4, pl. 3, figs. 2 & 3.

108. Two equestriennes
Gray pottery with white slip and pigments
19" (48 cm.) height of taller figure
Sui (581-618 AD) or early Tang Dynasty (618-906 AD)

109. Two equestrians
Gray pottery with white slip and pigment traces
14" (36 cm.) height of taller figure
Early Tang Dynasty (618-906 AD)

Comparative archaeological examples - similar figures were found in the early Tang tomb of Liu Kai and his wife, dated 664, at Yanshi, Henan province; see Wenwu, 1992, #12, p. 26, pls. 13-16.

110. Young camel with pack
Gray pottery with white slip and pigments
10" (25.5 cm.) high
Six Dynasties, Northern Wei period (386-535 AD)

111. Caparisoned horse
Gray pottery with white slip and pigments
9" (20.5 cm.) high
Six Dynasties (420-589 AD) or Sui Dynasty (581-618 AD)

Comparative archaeological examples - similar figures were found in the Northern Wei tomb of Yuan Shao, dated 528, at Luoyang, Henan province; see Kaogu, 1973, #4, pl. 11:1; and in the Northern Qi tomb of Gao Tan, dated 582, at Jing County, Hebei province; see Wenwu, 1979, #3, pl. 13:3.

112. Cart with ox and pig
Gray pottery with white slip and pigment traces
5" (13 cm.) height of cart
Eastern Han Dynasty (25-220 AD)

Comparative archaeological examples - a similar cart with an ox was found in an Eastern Han tomb; see Kaogu Tongxun, 1957, #1, pl. XIV:5.

113. Pair of officials
Gray pottery with white slip and pigment traces
5 1/4" (13 cm.) height of taller figure
Han Dynasty (206 BC-220 AD)

114. Cart and ox
Gray pottery
9 3/4" (25 cm.) height of cart
Six Dynasties, Northern Wei (386-535 AD) or Northern Qi period (550-577 AD)

Comparative archaeological examples - similar figures were found in the Northern Wei tomb, dated 524, at Quyang, Hebei province; see Kaogu, 1972, #5, pl. 3:2; and in the Northern Qi tomb of Prince Ruru, dated 550, at Dongchencun, Cixian, Hebei province; see Wenwu, 1984, #4, pl. 5:1. A similar cart was also found in the Northern Qi tomb at Taiyuan, Shanxi province; see Wenwu, 1990, #12, fig. 7.

115. Pack horse
Gray pottery
7 3/4" (19.5 cm.) high
Six Dynasties, Northern Wei period (386-535 AD)

Comparative archaeological examples - a similar figure was found in a Northern Wei tomb, dated 524, at Quyang, Hebei province; see Kaogu, 1972, #5, pl. 3:2.

116. Camel with pack
Gray pottery
11 3/4" (30 cm.) high
Six Dynasties, Northern Wei (386-535 AD) or Northern Qi period (550-577 AD)

Comparative archaeological examples - similar figures were found in a Northern Wei tomb, dated 524, at Quyang, Hebei province; see Kaogu, 1972, #5, pl. 3:2; and in the Northern Qi tomb of Prince Ruru, dated 550, at Dongchencun, Cixian, Hebei province; see Wenwu, 1984, #4, pl. 5:5.

117. Caparisoned horse
White pottery with pigments
12 1/2" (32 cm.) high
Sui Dynasty (581-618 AD)

Comparative archaeological examples - a very similar figure was found in a Sui tomb, datable to approximately

586, at Xijiao, Hefei, Anhui province; see Kaogu, 1976, #2, pp. 134-140, pl. 3:5

118. Four equestrian figures
White pottery with glazes and pigments
11" (28 cm.) height of tallest figure
Early Tang Dynasty (618-906 AD)

Comparative archaeological examples - similar figures were found in the Tang tomb of Zhang Shigui, dated 657, at Liquan, Shaanxi province; see Kaogu, 1978, #3, pp. 168-178, pl. 4:8-13, 5:3-4; and in the Tang tomb of Zheng Rentai, dated 664, at Xi'an, Shaanxi province; see Wenwu, 1972, #7, pp. 33-44, figs. 22-23.

119. Pair of archer equestrians
White pottery with yellow glaze and pigment traces
13 1/2" (34 cm.) high
Early Tang Dynasty (618-906 AD)

120. Archer equestrian
White pottery with yellow glaze and pigment traces
11 3/4" (29.5 cm.) high
Early Tang Dynasty (618-906 AD)

121. Pair of tomb guardian soldiers
White pottery with straw-colored glaze and pigment traces
15" (38 cm.) high
Sui (581-618 AD) or early Tang Dynasty (618-906 AD)

122. Ox
White pottery with straw-colored glaze and pigment traces
8" (20 cm.) high
Six Dynasties, Northern Qi period (550-577 AD)

Comparative archaeological examples - a similar figure was found in the Northern Qi tomb at Nanjiao, Taiyuan, Shanxi province; see Wenwu, 1990, #12, p. 9, fig. 3.

123. Attendant
10" (25.5 cm.) high
White pottery with straw-colored glaze and pigment traces
Sui (581-618 AD) or early Tang Dynasty (618-906 AD)

Comparative archaeological examples - a very similar figure was found in the Tang tomb of Zhang Shigui, dated 657, at Xi'an, Shaanxi province; see Kaogu, 1978, #3, pp. 168-178, pl. 1:8.

124. Bactrian camel
White pottery with straw-colored glaze and pigment traces
13 3/4" (35 cm.) high
Tang Dynasty (618-906 AD)

Comparative archaeological examples - a very similar figure was found in the Tang tomb of General Anpu and his wife, dated 709, at Luoyang, Henan province; see Zhongyuan Wenwu, 1982, #3, pp. 21-26, pl. 5:2.

125. Bactrian camel
White pottery with pigment traces
18 1/4" (46.5 cm.) high
Tang Dynasty (618-906 AD)

Comparative archaeological examples - a similar figure was found in the Tang tomb of Liu Kai and his wife, dated 664, at Yanshi, Henan province; see Wenwu, 1992, #12, p. 29, fig. 23.

126. Groom
White pottery with pigment traces
13 1/2" (34 cm.) high
Tang Dynasty (618-906 AD)

Comparative archaeological examples - an almost identical figure was found in the Tang tomb of Liu Kai and his wife, dated 664, at Yanshi, Henan province; see Wenwu, 1992, #12, pl. 8, fig. 2.

127. Prancing horse
White pottery with pigment traces
19 1/4" (49 cm.) high
Tang Dynasty (618-906 AD)

Comparative archaeological examples - a somewhat similar figure was found in the Tang tomb of General Yuanshou and his wife, dated 684-698, at Xi'an, Shaanxi province; see Wenwu, 1988, #12, p. 44, fig. 18.

128. Bactrian camel
White pottery with three-colored glazes
23" (58 cm.) high
Tang Dynasty (618-906 AD)

Comparative archaeological examples - a very similar figure was found in the Tang tomb of General Anpu and his wife, dated 709, at Luoyang, Henan province; see Zhongyuan Wenwu, 1982, #3, pp. 21-26, pls. 3:7-9.

129. Groom
White pottery with three-colored glazes
17 1/2" (54 cm.) high
Tang Dynasty (618-906 AD)

Comparative archaeological examples - very similar figures were found in the Tang tomb of Dugu Sizhen, dated 709, at Xi'an, Shaanxi province; see Tang Chang'an Chengjiao Suitangmu, pl. L, fig. 1 & 2 and pl. LXXXVII, fig. 3.

130. Horse
White pottery with brown glaze
20" (51 cm.) high
Tang Dynasty (618-906 AD)

Comparative archaeological examples - similar figures were found in the Tang tomb of Dugu Sizhen, dated 709, at Xi'an, Shaanxi province; see Tang Chang'an Chengjiao Suitangmu, pl. L, figs. 1 & 2.

131. Equestrian archer
White pottery with three-colored glazes
16 1/4" (41 cm.) high
Tang Dynasty (618-906 AD)

Comparative archaeological examples - very similar figures were found in the Tang tomb of General Anpu and his wife, dated 709, at Luoyang, Henan province; see Zhongyuan Wenwu, 1982, #3, pp. 21-26, pls. 4:1,2,4.

132. Court lady
White pottery with three-colored glazes
10 1/4" (26 cm.) high
Tang Dynasty (618-906 AD)

Comparative archaeological examples - very similar figures were found in the Tang tomb of General Anpu and his wife, dated 709, at Luoyang, Henan province; see Zhongyuan Wenwu, 1982, #12, pp. 21-25, pls. 5:7-9.

133. Foreign man playing a flute
Red pottery with white slip and yellow glaze
7 3/4" (19.5 cm.)
Tang Dynasty (618-906 AD)

134. Bactrian camel
White pottery with three-colored glazes
15 1/2" (39.5 cm.) high
Tang Dynasty (618-906 AD)

Comparative archaeological examples - very similar figures were found in the Tang tomb of General Anpu and his wife, dated 709, at Luoyang, Henan province; see Zhongyuan Wenwu, 1982, #3, pp. 21-26, pls. 3:7-9.

135. Groom
White pottery with three-colored glazes
12 1/4" (31 cm.) high
Tang Dynasty (618-906 AD)

Comparative archaeological examples - similar figures were found in the Tang tomb of General Anpu and his wife, dated 709, at Luoyang, Henan province; see Zhongyuan Wenwu, 1982, #3, pp. 21-26, pls. 3:7-9.

136. Equestrienne
White pottery with three-colored glazes
16 1/4" (41 cm.) high
Tang Dynasty (618-906 AD)

Comparative archaeological examples - a very similar figure was found in the Tang tomb of General Anpu and his wife, dated 709, at Luoyang, Henan province; see Zhongyuan Wenwu, 1982, #3, pp. 21-26, pls. 4:1-5.

137. Horse with saddle
White pottery with three-colored glazes
19 3/4" (50 cm.) high
Tang Dynasty (618-906 AD)

Comparative archaeological examples - similar figures were found in the Tang tomb of Princess Yongtai, dated 706, at Qianxian, near Xi'an, Shaanxi province; see Wenwu, 1964, #1, p. 11, fig. 5; and in a Tang tomb, dated 703, at Yanshi, Henan province; see Kaogu, 1992, #11, p. 1008, fig. 4:5.

138. Prancing horse
Red pottery with white slip
19 1/4" (49 cm.) high
Tang Dynasty (618-906 AD)

Comparative archaeological examples - a similar prancing horse, but made of white pottery and with a wavy mane, was found in the Tang tomb of Zhang Shigui, dated 657, at Xi'an, Shaanxi province; see Kaogu, 1978, #3, pp. 168-178, fig.

139. Dromedary camel with pack
Gray pottery with white slip
22" (56 cm.) high
Tang Dynasty (618-906 AD)

140. Cart and bull
Gray pottery with pigment traces
12" (30 cm.) height of cart
Tang Dynasty (618-906 AD)

Comparative archaeological examples - a very similar figure was found in the Tang tomb of Li Yanzhen, dated 685, at Xingyuancun, Yanshi, Henan province; see Kaogu, 1985, #10, pp. 904-914, fig. 6:6.

Mythical and Supernatural Beings

141. Lion
Earthenware with pigments
11" (28 cm.) high
Six Dynasties (386-581 AD)

142. Curled feline
Gray pottery with white slip and pigment traces
4" (9.5 cm.) high
Six Dynasties, Western Jin period (265-316 AD)

Comparative archaeological examples - a similar figure was found in an undated group of Wei-Jin tombs at Xingyuancun, Yanshi, Henan province; see Kaogu, #8, pp. 721-735, fig. 16.

143. Human-faced tomb guardian
Gray pottery with traces of white slip
10 1/2" (26.5 cm.) high
Six Dynasties, Northern Wei period (386-535 AD)

Comparative archaeological examples - a nearly identical figure was found in the Northern Wei tomb of Yuan Shao and his wife, dated 528, at Luoyang, Henan province; see Kaogu, 1973, #4, pp. 218-224, pl. 12:1.

144. Human-faced tomb guardian
Red pottery with pigment traces
15 1/2" (39.5 cm.) high
Six Dynasties, Northern Qi period (550-577 AD)

Comparative archaeological examples - very similar figures were found in a Northern Qi tomb, dated 550, at Cixian, Hebei province; see Wenwu, 1984, #4, p. 6, fig. 9; and in the Northern Qi tomb of Gao Run, dated 576, also at Cixian, Hebei province; see Kaogu, 1979, #3, p. 240, figs. 6:2-3.

145. Pair of human-faced tomb guardians
White pottery with straw-colored glaze
11" (28 cm.) high
Sui Dynasty (581-618 AD)

Comparative archaeological examples - a pair of similar figures, but with one having an animal face, was found in the Sui tomb, datable to approximately 586, at Xijiao, Hefei, Anhui province; see Kaogu, 1979, #2, pp. 134-140, pls. 1:1-2.

146. Fuxi and Nuwa
White pottery with pigment traces
8" (20 cm.) high
Early Tang Dynasty (618-906 AD)

Comparative archaeological examples - a very similar figure was found in the Tang tomb of Dong Man, dated 673, at Wen'anxian, Hebei province; see Wenwu, 1994, #1, pp. 84-93, pl. 16:4.

147. Fuxi and Nuwa
White pottery with pigment traces
6 1/2" (16.5 cm.) high
Early Tang Dynasty (618-906 AD)

Comparative archaeological examples - an identical figure was found in the Tang tomb, dated 668, at Donguguo, Nanhe, Hebei province; see Wenwu, 1993, #6, pp. 28-33, fig. 14.

148. Human-faced fish
Red pottery with pigment traces
4" (10 cm.) high
Early Tang Dynasty (618-906 AD)

Comparative archaeological examples - nearly identical figures were found in the Tang tomb of Dong Man, dated 673, at Wenanxian, Hebei province; see Wenwu, 1994, #1, pp. 84-93, pl. 16:2-3; in the Tang tomb of Guo Xiang at Nanhe, Hebei province; see Wenwu, 1993, #6, pp. 20-27, fig. 22; and in the Tang tomb at Dongguguo, Nanhe, Hebei province; see Wenwu, 1993, #6, pp. 28-33, fig. 13.

149. Two tomb guardians
White pottery with three-colored glazes
39" (100 cm.) height of taller figure
Tang Dynasty (618-906 AD)

Comparative archaeological examples - nearly identical figures were found in the Tang tomb of General Anpu and his wife, dated 709, at Luoyang, Henan province; see Zhongyuan Wenwu, 1982, #3, pp. 21-26, pls. 3:5-6; in the Tang tomb of Prince Zhanghuai, dated 706, near Xi'an, Shaanxi province; see Wenwu, 1972, #7, pp. 13-25, pl. 7; and in the Tang tomb of the Li Zhen, Prince of Yue, dated 718, at Liquan County, Shaanxi province; see Wenwu, 1977, #10, p. 45, fig. 9.

150. Two tomb guardians
Red pottery with white slip and pigment traces
18" (46 cm.) height of taller figure
Tang Dynasty (618-906 AD)

Comparative archaeological examples - identical figures were found in a group of Tang tombs at Xi'an, Shaanxi province; see Kaogu yu Wenwu, 1991, #4, p. 59, pl. 16:5-6.

151. Tomb guardian
Red pottery with white slip and extensive pigments
29" (74 cm.) high
Tang Dynasty (618-906 AD)

Comparative archaeological examples - a similar figure was found in a group of Tang tombs at Xi'an, Shaanxi province; see Kaogu yu Wenwu, 1991, #4, p. 60, fig. 17:2.

152. Two heavenly kings
White pottery with three-colored glazes
31" (79 cm.) high
Tang Dynasty (618-906 AD)

Comparative archaeological examples - very similar figures were found in the Tang tomb of General Anpu and his wife, dated 706, at Luoyang, Henan province; see Zhongyuan Wenwu, 1982, #3, pp. 21-26, pl. 3:2; and in a Tang tomb, dated 703, at Yanshi, Henan province; see Kaogu, 1992, #11, p. 1008, fig. 4:3-4.

153. Heavenly king
White pottery with pigment traces
41 1/2" (105.5 cm.) high
Tang Dynasty (618-906 AD)

Comparative archaeological examples - similar figures were found in the Tang tomb of Li Zhen, Prince of Yue, dated 718, at Liquan, Shaanxi; see Wenwu, 1977, #10, p. 44, figs. 5-6.

Bibliography

Akiyama, Terukazu et al. Arts of China: Neolithic Cultures to the T'ang Dynasty (Tokyo & Palo Alto: Kodansha, 1968).

Baker, Janet. Appeasing the Spirits: Sui and Tang Dynasty Tomb Sculpture from the Schloss Collection (Hofstra University Press, 1993).

Baker, Janet. "Appeasing the Spirits - Chinese Tomb Figures of the Sui and Early Tang Dynasty from the Schloss Collection," Minerva 1993, Vol. 4, #2, pp. 41-43.

Berger, Patricia. Ancestral Dwellings: Furnishing the Han Tomb (Asian Art Museum of San Francisco, 1987).

Berger, Patricia and Casler, Jennifer Randolph. Tomb Treasures from China, The Buried Art of Ancient Xi'an (Asian Art Museum of San Francisco, 1994).

Bush, Susan. "Thunder Monsters, Auspicious Animals, and Floral Ornament in Early Sixth-Century China," Ars Orientalis (1975, #10), pp. 19-33.

Capon, Edmund, Menzies, Jackie and Yang, Yang. Imperial China: The Living Past (Art Exhibitions Australia Limited, 1992).

Che, Mugi. The Silk Road: Past and Present (Beijing: Foreign Languages Press, 1989).

Chaves, Jonathan. "A Han Painted Tomb at Loyang," Artibus Asiae, 1968, Vol. 30, pp. 5-27.

Christy, Anita. "Articles of the Spirit - The Schloss Collection of Chinese Tomb Sculpture," Orientations, (August 1988), pp. 44-49.

Cotterell, Arthur. The First Emperor of China (New York: Holt, Rhinehart & Winston, 1981).

China Institute in America. Selections of Chinese Art from Private Collections (New York, 1987).

The Chinese Exhibition: A Pictorial Record of the Exhibition of Archaeological Finds of the People's Republic of China (The Nelson Gallery-Atkins Museum, 1974).

Dien, Albert E. "A Study of Early Chinese Armor," Artibus Asiae, 1981-1982, Vol. 43, 1,2, pp. 5-66.

Dien, Albert E. et al. The Quest for Eternity: Chinese Sculptures from the People's Republic of China (Los Angeles County Museum of Art, 1987).

Dunhuang Institute for Cultural Relics. Art Treasures of Dunhuang (Hong Kong: Joint Publishing, 1981).

Fine Chinese Ceramics and Works of Art (Sotheby's, New York, November 26, 1991).

Fong, Mary H. "Antecedents of Sui-Tang Burial Practices in Shaanxi," Artibus Asiae, 1991, Vol. 51, #3/4, pp. 147-198.

Fong, Mary H. "Four Chinese Royal Tombs of the Early Eighth Century," Artibus Asiae, 1973, Vol. 35, pp. 3-7-334.

Fong, Mary H. "Tomb-Guardian Figurines: Their Evolution and Iconography," Ancient Mortuary Traditions of China (LACMA, 1991).

Fontein, Jan and Wu, Tung. Unearthing China's Past (Boston Museum of Fine Arts, 1973).

Fontein, Jan and Wu, Tung. Han and T'ang Murals (Boston Museum of Fine Arts, 1976).

Gyllensvard, Bo and Pope, John Alexander. Chinese Art from the Collection of H.M. King Gustaf VI Adolf of Sweden (The Asia Society: Harry N. Abrams, Inc., 1966).

Hartman, Joan M. "Chinese Ceramic Sculpture in the Collection of Mr. and Mrs. Ezekiel Schloss," Oriental Art, 1969, Winter, Vol. 4.

Hawkes, David. Ch'u Tz'u: The Songs of the South (Oxford, 1959).

Hearn, Maxwell. Ancient Chinese Art: The Ernest Erickson Collection (Metropolitan Museum of Art, 1987).

Ho, Judy Chungwa. "Art and Context: Chinese Ceramic Sculpture," Orientations, (November 1989), pp. 62-69.
Important Chinese Ceramic Sculpture: Selected Masterpieces from the Schloss Collection (Sotheby's New York, December 3, 1984).

Juliano, Annette L. Art of the Six Dynasties: Centuries of Change and Innovation (China Institute, 1975).

Juliano, Annette L. Bronze, Clay and Stone: Chinese Art in the C.C. Wang Family Collection (University of Washington Press, 1988).

Juliano, Annette L. "Northern Dynasties: A Perspective," Chinese Archaic Bronzes, Sculpture and Works of Art (J.J. Lally & Co., New York, 1992).

Juliano, Annette L. Teng-Hsien: An Important Six Dynasties Tomb (Ascona, Switzerland: Artibus Asiae Publishers, 1980).

Kesner, Ladislav. "Portrait Aspects and Social Functions of Chinese Ceramic Tomb Sculpture," Orientations (Aug. 1991), pp. 33-42.

Lachman, Charles. Ming-ch'i Figures from the William E. Little Collection (Hood Museum of Art, Dartmouth College: 1989).

Lawton, Thomas et al. Asian Art in the Arthur M. Sackler Gallery: The Inaugural Gift, (Arthur M. Sackler Gallery, Smithsonian Institution, 1987).

Lee, George J. Selected Far Eastern Art in The Yale University Art Gallery (Yale University Press, 1970).

Lefebvre d'Argence, Rene-Yvon. Bronze Vessels of Ancient China in the Avery Brundage Collection (Asian Art Museum of San Francisco, 1977).

Lewis, Candace J. "Tall Towers of the Han," Orientations, (August 1990), pp. 45-54.

Lewis, Candace J. Into the Afterlife, Han and Six Dynasties Chinese Tomb Sculpture from the Schloss Collection (Vassar College Art Gallery, 1990).

Lim, Lucy (editor). Stories From China's Past: Han Dynasty Pictorial Tomb Reliefs and Archaelogical Objects from Sichuan Province (San Francisco, 1987).

Loewe, Michael. Chinese Ideas of Life and Death (London: Allen & Unwin, 1982).

Medley, Margaret. An Exhibition of Tang Sancai Pottery Selected from the Collection of Alan and Simone Hartman (London, 1988).

Neill, Mary Gardner. The Communion of Scholars: Chinese Art at Yale (China Institute in America, 1982).

Paludan, Ann. Chinese Tomb Figures (Oxford University Press, 1994).

Paludan, Ann. The Chinese Spirit Road: The Classical Tradition of Stone Tomb Statuary (Yale University Press, 1991)

Pirazzoli-t'Serstevens, Michele. The Han Dynasty, translated by Janet Seligman, (New York: Rizzoli, 1982).

Powers, Martin J. Art and Political Expression in Early China (Yale University Press, 1991).

Schafer, Edward. "Hunting Parks and Animal Enclosures in Ancient China," Journal of the Economic and Social History of the Orient, 1986, Vol. 11, pp. 318-343.

Schafer, Edward. The Golden Peaches of Samarkand (Berkeley and Los Angeles: University of California Press, 1963).

Schloss, Ezekiel. Ancient Chinese Ceramic Sculpture From Han Through T'ang (Castle Publishing, 1977).

Schloss, Ezekiel. Art of the Han (New York: China Institute in America, 1979).

Schloss, Ezekiel. Chinese Pottery Figurines (New York: China Institute in America, 1979).

Schloss, Ezekiel. Foreigners in Ancient Chinese Art (New York: China Institute in America, 1969).

Schloss, Ezekiel. Ming-ch'i: Clay Figures Reflecting Life in Ancient China (Katonah Gallery, 1975).

Sickman, Laurence and Alexander C. Soper. The Art and Architecture of China (Penguin Books, 1971).

Sickman, Laurence. "Chinese Painting Before 1100," Eight Dynasties of Chinese Painting (Cleveland Museum of Art, 1980), xiii-xxiv.

Soper, Alexander C. "South Chinese Influence on the Buddhist Art of the Six Dynasties Period," Bulletin of the Museum of Far Eastern Antiquities, Stockholm, 1960, no.32.

Steinhardt, Nancy S. Chinese Imperial City Planning (University of Hawaii, 1990).

Stepanchuk, Carol and Wong, Charles. Mooncakes and Hungry Ghosts: Festivals of China (San Francisco: China Books & Periodicals, 1991).

Thorp, Robert L. Son of Heaven: Imperial Arts of China (Son of Heaven Press, 1988).

Wang, Zhongshu. Han Civilization, translated by K.C. Chang and Collaborators (Yale University Press, 1982).

Watson, Burton. Chinese Lyricism: Shih Poetry from the Second to the Twelfth Century (New York: Columbia University Press, 1971).

Watson, William (editor). Pottery and Metalwork in T'ang China (London, 1970).

Watt, James C.Y. The Arts of Ancient China (Metropolitan Museum of Art, 1990).

Wen Fong (editor). The Great Bronze Age of China (Metropolitan Museum of Art, 1981).

White, Julia M. "Development of Objects of Personal Adornment in China," Adornment for Eternity: Status and Rank in Chinese Ornament (Denver Art Museum, 1994).

Wieger, L. Chinese Characters (Dover Publications, 1965).

Williams, C.A.S. Outlines of Chinese Symbolism and Art Motives (Charles E. Tuttle Co., Inc., 1974).

Wright, Arthur E. The Sui Dynasty (Knopf, 1978).

Wright, Arthur E. and Twitchett, Denis. Perspectives on the T'ang (Yale University Press, 1973).

Wu, Hung. "Buddhist Elements in Early Chinese Art" (2nd and 3rd Centuries A.D.), Artibus Asiae, 1986, Vol. 47, 3/4, pp. 263-303.

Wu Hung. The Wu Liang Shrine: The Ideology of Early Chinese Pictorial Art (Stanford University Press, 1989).

Young, Martie W. Early Chinese Ceramics From New York State Museums (New York: China Institute in America, 1991).

Yu, Ying-Shih. "Life and Immortality in the Mind of Han China," Harvard Journal of Asiatic Studies, 1964-65, Vol. 25, pp.80-122.

Sources In Chinese And Japanese

Archeological Excavation Team of Luoyang District. Luoyang Shaogou Hanmu (Han tombs at Shaogou, Luoyang), (Kexue Press, Beijing, 1959).

Cheng Qiren "Zailun Tangsancai Taoqi" ("Another Discussion of Tang Tricolor Ceramics") Lishi Wenwu (Historical Artifacts) 1995.8, pp. 17-24.

Chinese Archaeological Research Institute. Tang Chang'an Chengjiao Suitangmu (Sui and Tang Tombs in the Vicinity of the Tang City of Chang'an (Beijing: Wenwu Press, 1980).

Cultural Relics Bureau of the Ministry of Culture and the Palace Museum (editors). Quanguo Chutu Wenwu Zhenpin Chuan 1976-1984 (A Selection of the Treasure of Archaeological Finds of the People's Republic of China 1976-1984) (Beijing: Wenwu Press, 1985).

Dunhuang Research Institute. Dunhuang Mogaoku (Dunhuang Mogao Caves) Vol.II (Beijing: Wenwu Press, 1984).

Excavated Relics Exhibition Work Editors. Wenhua Dageming Shijian Qutu Wenwu (Cultural Relics Unearthed During the Cultural Revolution) (Beijing: Wenwu Press, 1973).

Hai Weilan. "Taotu Yibo Qingqianzai - Niuyue Schloss Fufu Jiqi Zhongguo Taomingqi Zangpin," ("A Rare Passion for Pottery: A Record of the New York Schloss Collection of Chinese Pottery Mingqi") Zhongguo Wenwu Shijie (Art of China), #77, 1992, pp. 28-57.

Hunan Provincial Museum and the Archaelogical Research Department of the Chinese Science Academy. Changsha Mawangdui Yihao Hanmu (The Number One Han Tomb at Mawangdui, Changsha, Hunan) 2 Vols., (Beijing, 1973).

Institute of Archaeology of the Chinese Academy of Science (editor). Huixian Fajue Baogao (Report on the Excavation at Huixian) (Beijing: Kexue Press, 1956).

Lin Shuxin." Tangsancai Zhenpin Shangxi" ("An Appreciation of Tang Tri-color Treasures") Lishi Wenwu (Historical Artifacts) 1995.8, pp. 12-16.

Liu, Dunzhao, et. al. Zhongguo Gudai Jianzhushi (A History of Ancient Chinese Architecture) (Beijing: Chinese Architectural Press, 1984).

Liu Zhiyuan, et al. Sichuan Handai Huaxiangzhuan yu Handai Shehui (Han Dynasty Pictorial Tomb Tiles and Han Dynasty Society) (Beijing: Wenwu Press, 1983).

Nagahiro, Toshio. Kandai Gazo no Kenkyu (The Representational Art of the Han Dynasty), in Japanese with English summary, (Tokyo, 1965).

Osaka Municipal Museum. Kinryu, Kinba to Dobutsu Kokuhoten (National Treasures Exhibition of Golden Dragons, Golden Horses and Other Animals) (Osaka, 1987).

Osaka Municipal Museum. Zui To no Bijutsu (Art of the Sui and Tang) (Heibonsha, 1978).

Shanxi Provincial Cultural Relics Preservation Institute. Yungang Shiku (Yungang Caves) (Beijing: Wenwu Press, 1977).

Shaanxi Provincial Museum. Sui Tang Wenhua (Sui and Tang Culture) (Hong Kong: China Publishing, 1990).

Shaanxi Provincial Museum. Tang Li Chongjun Mubihua (Murals in the Tang Tomb of Li Chongjun) (Beijing: Wenwu Press, 1974).

Shaanxi Provincial Museum. Tang Li Xian Mubihua (Murals in the Tang Tomb of Li Xian) (Beijing: Wenwu Press, 1974).

Shaanxi Provincial Museum. Tangmu Bihua Zhenpin Xuancui (The Cream of Original Frescoes From Tang Tombs) (Shaanxi People's Art Publishing House, 1991).

Sung, Kee-in. "Tangrende Shenghuo Yu Yishu" ("The Life-Style and Art of the Tang Dynasty") Lishi Wenwu (Historical Artifacts) 1993.6, pp. 57-67.

Tao Qian and Gu Bing. Liuchao Yishu (Art of the Six Dynasties) (Beijing: Wenwu Press, 1981).

Tao Qian and Gu Bing. Nanbei Lingmu Shike (Stone Carving of the Six Dynasties) (Beijing: Wenwu Press, 1981).

Xinjiang Provincial Museum. Sichou Zhilu: Han Tang Zhiwu (The Silk Route: Han and Tang Textiles) (Beijing: Wenwu Press, 1973).

Zeng Zhaoju, Jiang Baogeng and Li Zhongyi. Yinan Gu Huaxiang Shi Mu Fajue Baogao (The Excavation Report on the Ancient Stone Tomb with Wall Paintings at Yinan), (Cultural Relics Bureau of the Ministry of Culture, 1956).

Zheng Zhende (editor). Quanguo Jiben Jianshe Gongzheng Zhong Chutu Wenwu Zhanlan Tulu (Illustrated Catalogue of the Cultural Relics Excavated at Construction Sites Nationwide), 2 Vols., (Shanghai, 1954.)

Zhongguo Lidai Fushi (Chinese Historical Costumes) (Shanghai Art Press, 1984).

Zhou Dao et al. Henan Handai Huaxiangzhuan (Henan Pictorial Tomb Tiles of the Han Dynasty) (Shanghai People's Art Press, 1985).

Archaeological Reports

Kaogu, 1955, #4, pp. 54-56 (A Tang tomb at Dasi Kongcun, Anyang).

Kaogu, 1959, #6, pp. 285-287 (The excavation of a Northern Dynasties tomb at Caochangpo Village in the southern suburbs of Xi'an).

Kaogu, 1959, #8, pp. 419-429 (A brief report on the cleaning of an ancient tomb at the irrigation canal at Mumashan, Sichuan).

Kaogu, 1959, #9 (A report on the discovery of the Sui tomb of Li Jingxun at Xian).

Kaogu, 1959, #10, pp. 541-545 (A report on the discovery of the Sui tomb of Zhang Sheng at Anyang).

Kaogu, 1959, #12, pp. 662-667 (A brief report of the second excavation of the Qin and Han tombs at Hongqing Village, Chang'an, Shaanxi).

Kaogu, 1965, #4, pp. 209-211 (A Jin tomb at the village of Sanmao, Yicheng county, Jiangsu).

Kaogu, 1966, #3, pp. 130-137 (A tomb at Gulugou, Xinan County, Henan).

Kaogu, 1972, #5, pp. 33-35 (A Northern Wei tomb discovered at Quyang, Hebei).

Kaogu, 1973, #4, pp. 218-224 (The Northern Wei tomb of Yuan Shao at Luoyang).

Kaogu, 1975, #2, pp. 116-123 (A brief report on the excavation of an Eastern Han tomb at Qilihe, Jianxi, Luoyang).

Kaogu, 1976, #2, pp. 129-133 (The excavation of the pits for funerary objects accompanying a Han mausoleum at Renjiapo, Xi'an).

Kaogu, 1976, #2, pp. 134-140 (A Sui tomb at Xijiao, Hefei).

Kaogu, 1977, #5, pp. 313-326 (A Brief Report on the Tang tomb of Li Feng).

Kaogu, 1977, #6, pp. 391-402 (An Eastern Wei tomb at Dongchencun, Cixian, Hebei).

Kaogu, 1978, #3, pp. 168-178 (The Tang tomb of Zhang Shigui at Liquan, Shaanxi).

Kaogu, 1979, #3, pp. 235-244 (The Northern Qi tomb of Gao Run at Cixian, Hebei).

Kaogu, 1981, #5, pp. 422-425 (The investigation of the Han Anling and the painted ceramic figures in its satellite tombs).

Kaogu, 1983, #9, pp. 793-798 (A report on the discovery of a Sui tomb at Yuejiazui, Donghu District, Wuhan).

Kaogu, 1985, #5, pp. 429-449 (A Han tomb at Laodaosi, Mian County, Shaanxi).

Kaogu, 1985, #8, pp. 721-735 (Two Wei-Jin period tombs at Xingyuan Village, Yanshi, Henan).

Kaogu, 1985, #10, pp. 904-914 (Two Tang tombs at Xingyuancun, Yanshi, Henan).

Kaogu, 1985, #12, pp. 429-449 (A Han tomb at Laodaosi, Mian County, Shaanxi).

Kaogu, 1992, #1 pp. 32-45 (A report on the discovery of two Sui tombs at Anyang City, Henan).

Kaogu, 1992, #1, (A Tang tomb with a folding stone casket platform discovered in Tianshui, Gansu).

Kaogu Tongxun, 1955, #2, pp. 33-40 (A brief report on the archeological excavations in the neighborhood of Baoji and Xi'an, Shaanxi Province).

Kaogu Tongxun, 1955, #2, pp. 40-45 (A brief report on the excavation of a Six Dynasties tomb at Bishanzhong, Wuxi, Jiangsu Province).

Kaogu Tongxun, 1955 #5, pp. 43-49 (A brief report on the cleaning up of some Jin dynasty tombs in the northwestern suburbs of Guangzhou).

Kaogu Tongxun, 1955 #6, pp. 32-39 (A brief report on the cleaning of a Han dynasty tomb at Pujizhen, Zhangqiuxian, Shangdong).

Kaogu Tongxun, 1956, #4, pp. 12-17 (A brief report of the cleaning of an Eastern Han tomb at Dongshan, Guangzhou).

Kaogu Tongxun, 1956, #4, pp. 40-42 (The discovery of a Southern Dynasties tomb at Zhuanshishan, Nanjing).

Kaogu Tongxun, 1957, #1, pp. 37-41 (An account of the excavation of the Jin dynasty tomb at Zhengzhou, Henan).

Kaogu Tongxun, 1957, #3, pp. 28-37 (A report on the investigation of the Feng family cluster of tombs in Jingxian, Hebei).

Kaogu Tongxun, 1957, #4, pp. 9-19 (A brief report on the excavation of the Han and Tang burials at Liujiaqu, Shanxian, Henan Province in 1956).

Kaogu Xuebao, 1958, #1, pp. 87-103 (The record of the inspection of the mountain cliff tombs at Tianhui, Chengdu).

Kaogu Xuebao, 1965, #1, p.132 (A brief report on the excavation of a Han tomb at Liujiaqu, Shan county, Henan).

Kaogu Xuebao, 1979, #3, pp. 377-401 (The Northern Qi tomb of Kudi Huilo).

Kaogu Xuebao, 1990, #4, pp. 475-496 (A Han tomb with pictorial bricks at Xinye, Fanji, Henan).

Kaogu yu Wenwu, 1981, #2, pp. 21-24 (A record of the inspection of the Western Wei tomb at Cuijiaying, Hanzhong City).

Kaogu yu Wenwu, 1982, #2 (A brief report on the excavation of Han tomb no. 4 at Laodaosi, Mian County, Shaanxi).

Kaogu yu Wenwu, 1991, #4, pp. 50-95 (A report on the cleaning of Sui and Tang tombs at the heat and power plant construction site in the western outskirts of Xi'an).

Wenwu, 1960, #8-9, pp. 19-24 (The excavation of Han tomb no. 159 at Nanguan, Zhengzhou).

Wenwu, 1961, #1, pp. 56-66 (A brief account of the excavation of a group of Han dynasty tombs of the Yang family at Diaochao, Tongguan, Shaanxi).

Wenwu, 1964, #1, pp. 7-33 (A report on the discovery of the Tang tomb of Princess Yongtai).

Wenwu, 1966, #3, pp. 1-5 (A large quantity of Western Han painted earthernware funerary sculptures excavated at Yangjiawan, Xianyang, Shaanxi Province).

Wenwu, 1966, pp. 59-60 (Introducing a late Eastern Han earthenware water-side pavilion).

Wenwu, 1966, #1, pp. 27-43 (A report on the cleaning of the Sui tomb of Li He at Shuangchengcun, Sanyuanxian, Shaanxi).

Wenwu, 1972, #1, pp. 47-51 (A report on the discovery of the Northern Qi tomb of Fan Cui at Anyang, Henan).

Wenwu, 1972, #2, pp. 70-72 (A group of Han dynasty cultural relics unearthed in recent years in Wuzhou city, Guangxi).

Wenwu, 1972, #3, pp. 20-33, 64 (The Northern Wei tomb of Sima Jinlong at Shijiazhai, Datong, Shanxi).

Wenwu, 1972, #7 pp. 13-21 (A report on the discovery of the Tang tomb of Prince Zhanghuai).

Wenwu, 1972, #7, pp. 26-31 (A report on the discovery of the Tang tomb of Prince Yide).

Wenwu, 1972, #7, pp. 33-41 (A report on the discovery of the Tang tomb of Zheng Rentai).

Wenwu, 1972, #10, pp. 41-48 (A Han dynasty tomb with pictorial hollow bricks at Xintongqiao, Zhengzhou, Henan).

Wenwu, 1972, #10, pp. 49-62 (Han Dynasty tombs with the painted stone walls and mural paintings at Dahuting, Mixian, Henan).

Wenwu, 1973, #2, pp. 46-53 (The excavation of three Han tombs at Sijian'gou, Jiyuan).

Wenwu, 1973, #2, pp. 55-60 (An Eastern Han sacrificial tomb at Dongguan, Luoyang).

Wenwu, 1973, #4, pp. 21-35 (A Western Han cliff tomb at Xiaoguishan, Tongshan, Jiangsu).

Wenwu, 1974, #1, pp. 8-23 (The discovery of an important Eastern Han tomb with mural paintings at Holinge'er, Inner Mongolia).

Wenwu, 1974, #2, pp. 15-26 (A brief report on the discovery of bamboo slips recording the {Sun Zi Bing Fa}, etc. from a Western Han tomb at Linyi, Shandong).

Wenwu, 1974, #2, pp. 36-40 (A wooden coffin of the Warring States period at Zidanku, Changsha).

Wenwu, 1974, #2, p. 70 (A painted pottery granary tower unearthed from an Eastern Han tomb in Jiaozuo, Henan).

Wenwu, 1974, #6, pp. 41-61 (A brief report on the excavation of the Western Han tomb at Fenghuangshan, Jiangling, Hubei).

Wenwu, 1974, #9, pp. 71-88 (A brief report on the discovery of the Tang tomb of Li Shou).

Wenwu, 1975, #4, pp. 64-73 (A Northern Qi tomb at Baigu, Qixian, Shanxi).

Wenwu, 1975, #9, pp. 1-19 (A brief report on the excavation of Han tomb no. 168 at Fenguangshan, Jiangling, Hubei).

Wenwu, 1975, #10, pp. 75-93 (Late Eastern Han tombs at Zhangwan, Lingbao County, Henan Province).

Wenwu, 1975, #11, pp. 75-93 (The Han tombs at Lingbao, Zhangwan, Henan).

Wenwu, 1977, #10, pp. 50-59 (Memorial tablets and imperial edicts excavated in the Tang royal tombs at Lingchuan).

Wenwu, 1977, #10, pp. 10-21 (A brief report on the excavation of the Han tomb at Yangjiawan, Xianyang).

Wenwu, 1977, #11 pp. (The excavation of Han tomb no.9 at Jinjueshan, Linyi County, Shandong Province).

Wenwu, 1979, #1, pp. 82-91 (The evolution of the species of domesticated pigs as seen in China's excavated cultural relics).

Wenwu, 1979, #2, p. 94 (The Han dynasty green-glazed pottery tower unearthed at Xiangyang, Hubei).

Wenwu, 1979, #3, pp. 17-29 (A report on the discovery of the Northern Wei Gao family tombs at Jingxian, Hebei).

Wenwu, 1981, #4, pp. 28-33 (A report on the cleaning of Sui tomb #1 at Yingshan, Jiaxiang, Shandong).

Wenwu, 1981, #4, pp. 39-43 (A Sui tomb of the Sixth Year of Daye at Xiangyinxian, Hunan).

Wenwu, 1983, #10, pp. 1-23 (A report on the discovery of the Northern Qi tomb of Lou Rui at Taiyuan).

Wenwu, 1984, #4, pp. 16-22 (A Northern Qi tomb at Dongchencun, Cixian, Hebei).

Wenwu, 1984, #4, pp. 1-9 (A report on the discovery of the tomb of Eastern Wei Ruru at Cixian, Hebei).

Wenwu, 1987, #8, pp. 43-51 (The Tang tomb of Cui Na in the Northern suburbs of Changzhi, Shanxi).

Wenwu, 1988, #12, pp. 37-49 (A report on the discovery of the Tang tomb of An Yuanshou and his spouse.).

Wenwu, 1990, #7, pp. 43-45 (A Tang tomb in the Western Suburb of Xian).

Wenwu, 1990, #12, pp. 1-10 (A Northern Qi tomb with murals in the southern suburbs of Taiyuan, Shanxi).

Wenwu, 1992, #3, pp. 1-8 (A Tang tomb at Xishantou, Mengjin, Luoyang).

Wenwu, 1992, #4, pp. 1-13 (The number one brief report on the discovery of the accessory burial pit in the Southern area of the Yangling Tomb of Han Jingdi).

Wenwu, 1992, #9, pp. 66-70 (A Tang tomb in the Western suburb of Xian at the Red Flag Power Plant).

Wenwu, 1992, #12, pp. 1-8 (A brief report on the clearing of a Han tomb with murals at Xinmang Yanshi, Luoyang, Henan).

Wenwu, 1992, #16, pp. 1-14 (A brief report on the cleaning of the tomb of Luche at Taiyuan).

Wenwu, 1993, #6, pp. 20-27 (The Tang tomb of Guo Xiang at Nanhe, Hebei).

Wenwu, 1993, #6, pp. 28-33 (The Tang tomb at Dongguguo, Nanhe, Hebei).

Wenwu, 1994, #1, pp. 84-93 (A Tang tomb at Magezhuang, Wen'an County, Hebei).

Wenwu, 1992, #12, pp. 21-33 (The Tang tomb of Liukai at Yanshi, Henan).

Zhongyuan Wenwu, 1982, #3, pp. 21-26, 14 (The Tang tomb of An Pu and his spouse at Longmen, Luoyang).